Virtuous Living

Fulfilling your individual purpose in life

First published by O Books, 2009
O Books is an imprint of John Hunt Publishing Ltd., The Bothy, Deershot Lodge, Park Lane, Ropley,
Hants, SO24 0BE, UK
office1@o-books.net
www.o-books.net

Distribution in:	South Africa
	Alternative Books
UK and Europe	altbook@peterhyde.co.za
Orca Book Services	Tel: 021 555 4027 Fax: 021 447 1430
orders@orcabookservices.co.uk	
Tel: 01202 665432 Fax: 01202 666219	Text copyright Belinda Joubert 2008
Int. code (44)	
	Design: Stuart Davies
USA and Canada	
NBN	ISBN: 978 1 84694 195 5
custserv@nbnbooks.com	
Tel: 1 800 462 6420 Fax: 1 800 338 4550	All rights reserved. Except for brief quotations
	in critical articles or reviews, no part of this
Australia and New Zealand	book may be reproduced in any manner without
Brumby Books	prior written permission from the publishers.
sales@brumbybooks.com.au	
Tel: 61 3 9761 5535 Fax: 61 3 9761 7095	The rights of Belinda Joubert as author have
	been asserted in accordance with the
Far East (offices in Singapore, Thailand,	Copyright, Designs and Patents Act 1988.
Hong Kong, Taiwan)	
Pansing Distribution Pte Ltd	
kemal@pansing.com	A CIP catalogue record for this book is available
Tel: 65 6319 9939 Fax: 65 6462 5761	from the British Library.

Printed by Digital Print

O Books operates a distinctive and ethical publishing philosophy in
all areas of its business, from its global network of authors to
production and worldwide distribution.
This book is produced on FSC certified stock, within ISO14001
standards. The printer plants sufficient trees each year through
the Woodland Trust to absorb the level of emitted carbon in
its production.

Virtuous Living

Fulfilling your individual purpose in life

Belinda Joubert

BOOKS

Winchester, UK
Washington, USA

CONTENTS

Foreword

Belinda wrote this book to tell the desperate people of the world that there is hope and blessings for all, when we know where to look and know how to access it. It does not matter how dark our hour is. There is always light in our darkest hour when we retain our enthusiasm for life. There is absolutely no reason for desperation and hopelessness in our lives.

When people experience adversity, it is a special course in a special wisdom that we required. Once we have learnt the intended lesson, we have added another skill insight to our quiver of mastery. We all have all the solutions to our problems within us, because we are spiritual fragments of God, giving us access to His infinite virtuous wisdom.

We always tend to intellectualize the road of a virtuous life, when all we need to do is believe in a few simple natural laws, formulated for us thousands of years ago by minds that interacted with God. We have access to these wisdoms every day by stilling our minds and listening to the voice messages of our heart, which God may have sent us.

This book helped Belinda and our family to find and describe the way that we seemed to miss when we were ignorant of the simple ways of God. To many people the road of a virtuous life is the one less traveled. When more people travel this road, the road will become easier and safer, with more people being able to help those who experience a breakdown. I trust that you will also travel on this road and experience the wonderful experiences and insights that this road offers to travelers.

Daniel A Joubert
Talent Management Coach

Dedication

To the magnificence of the modern man and women who are sufficiently broad in their thinking to adopt new methods to achieve success and happiness through honoring the Creators Natural Supreme Laws and by living a life of virtue.

I dedicate this book to YOU, the reader. May the spirit within you awaken and turn you into a true Lightworker. This book will guide you to self-mastery and the fulfillment of your individual purpose of life, giving love and service to God's creations and humanity. This book will help you to grow your soul and to prepare you for eternity when you move onto the next plane of life.

The only way to develop self is to forget self. The more you think of others, the better self you will become. S Birch

Acknowledgements

Thank you to Spirit Who has blessed and embraced me with His infinite love through sharing the information in this book with me to make a difference in the world of matter. I strive to be a person from the Light and to live in harmony and balance with my work and special talents. I humbly wish to make a positive difference in the life of others by sharing and spreading the information shared with me. My earnest thank you to the Higher Power, which gave me guidance and insights to continue along my path.

Virtuous Living is a special creation of the guidance, love and blessings from Raphael my Guardian Angel, Silver Birch one of my spiritual guides and all my other guides and helpers who daily embraced me with the ability to hear the inner guidance from the Highest Power and therefore I am truly grateful.

My sincere thank you to John Hunt my publisher. John you are a noble Lightworker! From the very beginning, you believed in Virtuous Living and you overwhelmed me with your confidence and trust that we will be able to share the insights in this book with humanity. You are truly profound, may God shower you with abundant love and blessings.

A book is only as good as the team behind it. My honest thank you to the O-Books team for the effort that you all have put into making this book the exquisite book that it is. The love and effort from the designing of the cover to the final product takes hours of sincere love and support, thank you for every individual on the team who was part of this final lovely product.

Thank you to Ilze who has turned the images into lovely works of art. Ilze you are one of the most positive, inspiring and creative individuals that I know. Thank you for being you. You are always available to walk the extra mile.

A warm thank you to my husband Danie who is my soulmate and my sun and who uplifts me, you are the reason that I am able to spread my wings and pursue my truest passion. Danie thank you for your continuous love and support. To my lovely children Lizél, Charl, Daniëlle and Serena Elizabeth, you are always my greatest supporters and inspiration, I love you all.

Sometimes God blesses you with special friends that come into your life at the divine time and makes your heart swell with gratitude and wonder, such friends are Simoné, Gerda, Miems, Lesley, Tertia and Marieta. I am honored that God has placed you all on my path of development. Miems in your quiet way, you always know what to feed my soul to inspire me. Simoné you are God's truest, greatest Lightworker. I love you dearly! Gerda you are the mastermind and my shining star, I nurture you in my heart. To Lesley, you are always there for me, solid as the rock of Gibraltar. You always give love graciously and shower humanity with kindness; we all can learn from you how to be a Lightworker. Thank you for your wisdom and guidance, I love you all dearly!

To my sister Tertia and my dear friend Marieta you fill a special place in my heart, you are gemstones. You two are always there for me.

About the Author

Belinda specializes in inspirational workshops, lectures and teaching individuals how to do card readings to unite with Source. Her paramount vision is to assist individuals to open the correct channels and to connect with Shekinah our Godly presence. She aspires to help individuals to become Lightworkers. Belinda is also a public and inspirational speaker, with an offering of inspirational and spiritual card decks such as angels, fairies, nature wisdom and others. Her professional career started as a high-school teacher. She has a Higher Education Diploma (THOD), a Diploma in Marketing and Marketing Research, a Certificate in Public Relations Practice and completed a Graduate Programme in Utility Management with the USA Stanford Business School.

Belinda Joubert is also the founder and managing director of Inspire Achievement Solutions (Pty) Ltd. The company offers employee vitality solutions to individuals, executives, professionals and companies and institutions. These customized interventions ignite and inspire the human spirit within and help individuals to build and experience a virtuous life in the innate presence of Divine Spirit.

She worked several years for a public enterprise and fulfilled various executive roles in public relations and marketing before she founded her company. She won several awards for top performance in her field. During her years in the corporate world, she sensed and experienced the spiritual barrenness of the workplace and she decided to dedicate her life to her truest interest, which is the origin and meaning of spirituality and the influence of spirituality and the natural laws for virtuous living on human behavior in society and the workplace. She explores folklore, spiritual truths and ancient writings about spiritual and divine phenomena and the dynamics of God's divine universe and seeks to expand human understanding of these phenomena unrestrained by popular religions or spiritual dogmas, thus her first book AngelSense was born.

Belinda published the book AngelSense in 2006. The publication of AngelSense heralds a profound milestone in her personal spiritual evolvement and teaching career. The central theme is the personae of God's divine messengers and their influences on our lives.

Virtuous Living assists individuals with self-actualization and preparation for eternity. Virtuous Living will advise individuals on how to live a balanced lifestyle by applying and living in harmony with the natural laws. At some stage of development during our lifetime, we experience feelings as if lost within a maze, Virtuous Living will give guidance, light, hope and comfort to souls who experience such feelings. When individuals connect with Source they are able to live on all aspects of being, spiritually, mentally and physically.

www.inspirationalcardsandgifts.com

www.angelsense.net

Mobile: 082 855 6899

Introduction

Whenever you have truth it must be given with love, or the message and the messenger will be rejected.
Mahatma Gandhi

We all have to strive to be ambassadors of the Divine and to make the world a better place for all of God's creations. We are spiritual beings and in miniature, we are a tiny fraction of God. Our purpose in life is to live fully on all aspects of our being, spiritually, mentally and physically.

We are on earth to build our character and we have to grow our souls to prepare for eternity. We can accomplish this through cultivating the fruits of spirit, which are love, joy, peace, forgiveness, gentleness, goodness, compassion, graciousness and faith.

We must always strive to be kinder than necessary because everyone we meet is fighting some kind of battle. There is so much violence, hatred, confusion, misery, conflict and heartache in our daily lives. Too many individuals live in the darkness of fear, poverty, superstition and ignorance.

One of our most important tasks in life is to give love and service to individuals who are unhappy, poor, distressed, out of balance, lost and fearful. We have to touch souls and we have to help to spread the light. We have to help souls to grow, develop and unfold. In the highly competitive physical world today materialism rules and it is the biggest cancer of the world.

It is Spirit that gives life and we need to guide individuals to embrace the Holy Ghost into their lives. We have to learn to cultivate confidence, trust, faith, peace and tranquility within to create the perfect conditions for the Divine Power to be able to enter our hearts, minds and souls.

When you embrace the spirit within, you live a virtuous life. You have accomplished moral excellence, which means your character's essence is built on integrity, honesty, rectitude, ethics and decent behavior. In other words, you are honoring God's divine, natural, supreme laws and you are helping others. You are like a little lighthouse that offers direction and spreads the light.

Our Creator has equipped us with our reason, which connects us to God. All the answers that you seek are born within your own thoughts. To fulfill your individual purpose in life you have be aware of the basic essential periods of human life, divided into primary seven-year cycles. You must be aware of the Twenty-Two states of consciousnesses in these seven-year cycles. They link with your continuous life's journey and teach you about spiritual wellness. These stages and states of consciousnesses link to the energy centers or chakras within you. All are interlinked and connected with Spirit.

If we follow these few basic principles daily and choose to be a Lightworker, it is possible to live a virtuous, *perfect* life. Then we light up the darkness and we build our character towards preparing for eternity.

Part I

Who you are is a necessary step to being who you will be.
Emmanuel

Chapter 1

Understand Reality and Purpose of Life

To understand your existence and purpose in life, you have to go through the cycles of life. Life sometimes appears to be difficult, full of heartache, confusion, conflict and violence. Each one of us is seeking some relief, some happiness and a way out of the darkness into the light. Our current reality in our daily lives has its moments and its effects of discourse and disgruntlement. Where to from here, you might think, and ask? Is there an answer? Yes! You are the answer. The great *Mahatma Gandhi* reminded us that *you have to be the change so the change can happen in your life.* The secret is that the answer begins with the core, and with what you think that will manifest the changes in your life. Where does one discover the inner-inner essence of it all? We search for the purpose of life, the true beauty of life by focusing on the material things in life. Unfortunately, we devote all our efforts to gain attachments and possessions far beyond what we need and by doing so sacrifice our eternal realities. Our eternal realities are the greatest asset that humanity can have.

Our real purpose in life lies within ourselves (meaning how to find the right career in which you can accomplish and fulfill yourself and make a difference to humanity and give service to God). You are the vessel that holds the knowledge.

If you are lonely, miserable, depressed, sad, unhappy or lost, not knowing where to turn to, you are at a turning point in your life. Begin today to follow a few simple rules to manifest whatever you desire. God's natural laws cannot fail, they have never failed, but we have to make them come alive in our lives. Turning within and surrendering to your Higher Self will give you the answers you seek. You are in charge of you, and you

11

know instinctively that there is a higher power beyond, in which we live and move and have our being. Focus on a message of thought that will engage and enhance you to the level of attainment that you need right this moment. Balance and align yourself with your purest of thoughts and activate them into a measurement that will engage many new vibrations of action. It is letting go and letting God take over your life. You have to regenerate yourself. You have to find yourself and your purpose. You have to change your own heart, your own mind and your outlook, so that the spirit, which is divine, finds the fullest expression. You have started your spiritual journey... *You are bathed in the radiance of the divine light, which is always yours.* S. Birch

When your soul awakens to the realities of life, you can attain spiritual wellness, which means you are living a life of virtue and integrity by giving service to mankind and by uplifting souls.

You are fulfilling yourself when you allow the Spirit to manifest in your life and when your soul awakens to the realities in life - then you are at peace with yourself and with Spirit. You have to begin to exercise true harmony of being, which is the fundamental purpose of your life on earth. You will find your way, once the soul comes into its own and you realize its true power.

Chapter 2

Your Individual Purpose in Life

The whole purpose of your earthly life is that you live on all aspects of your being. You need to sustain balance- spiritually, mentally, and physically.

Get the proper perspective, you are a spiritual being. You are a special being from the Light and the Divine Spark is within you. Only you can find this spiritual truth and make it a reality in your life. You have to find the knowledge. You cannot learn spiritual lessons through a substitute. You cannot gain spiritual lessons through cheating or bribery. You cannot buy spiritual lessons. You can only attain and concur with life's lessons through experience. You only learn through suffering, pain, sadness, hardship and extreme adversity. You have to seek spiritual truths through life experiences, events, trial and error, circumstances, reading, learning, religion, philosophy and science. You have to find knowledge and the light within your heart. You have to make a decision and refuse to live in ignorance, superstition and darkness. You have to grow your soul.

The whole purpose of your earthly life is that you live on all aspects of your being. You need to sustain balance- spiritually, mentally, and physically. You are not fulfilling yourself unless you have perfect harmony between your spirit, mind and body. You will experience wellness and health when you live correctly, when your thinking is right and when your body, mind and spirit are in synergy.

You as the soul know before it incarnates what it has to do. You have a contract or blueprint and do not start your physical existence as a spirit without any awareness of itself. You, as the

13

spirit choose the vehicle, your physical body and specific combination of circumstances of your incarnation. The spirit knows that the combination of circumstances will provide the best opportunities for the necessary unfoldment it has to undergo. Know that you have divine power within you and that you can rise above any circumstance. When the spirit incarnates into a physical body, the complexity of the state of being, prevents the awareness, which is, embedded deep down, from reaching your consciousness. For this reason, we look at life from the wrong perspective and focus only on material possessions. You have to realize that life is not only earthly and material. Life is spiritual and eternal.

There is a Divine Plan, but you have to realize that the Divine Plan is not rigid and that you have to play your part. You are not a puppet. You are a part of the Divine Spirit, which portrays the divine inspiration within. *You have personal responsibility and a measure of free will, but not so great that you can counteract the operation of the natural laws.* S. Birch. Within the scope of the natural law, you have the power to choose and act. Your supreme destiny is fixed, but it is for you to unfold and develop your latent divinity with the blueprint that you have. You have agreed on this blueprint before your incarnation, but you may not consciously be aware of this or remember this agreement. Subconsciously you have an urge for soul- growth. Your soul, because it is divine, is restless, rushing forward and striving to express itself. You are determined and motivated to grow. The soul comes into its own through adverse experiences such as suffering, sadness, distress, illness or mourning. This is one of God's fundamental natural laws and you have to experience adversity in some other form to experience soul- growth. You cannot have it any other way - it is the only way. You have to experience the feeling and have the emotion. Only when the heart is stirred, you as a spiritual being, are open to receive the higher vibration of the Cosmic Consciousness. Locked within your soul is an energy greater that any energy know on earth. This energy is part of God. Without this energy, there could be no life, for life is Spirit (God). Spirit expresses itself through you, and Spirit has created you, you can always draw upon this invisible wellspring, which loves and guides and protects you. Spirit knows you and Spirit is your infinite Source and supply of supreme energy.

In a world filled with disappointment and terror, where millions are fearful of tomorrow, it is important that you understand what life truly is. Not life on the surface but life's reality - it is important that you are aware that you are an infinite soul and that your stay on earth is a small but necessary part of an eternal life. You must go through your apprenticeship on earth before you qualify to move on to the spiritual plane. The plan of life is very simple. You have to go through experiences on earth to prepare you to move on for the tasks and the joys that awaits you on the spiritual plane. You have to equip yourself with the sufficient experiences before you can do your work. Earth is like the school and you learn all the lessons, which prepare you for the life after school. Remember soul-mastery is not easy. There are no short cuts to supremacy and no beds of roses. Think of the classical example of the ballerina with toes full of blisters, blood and calluses. Your reward is a spiritual adventure filled with happiness, excitement and wonder!

Silver Birch explains our individual purpose in life as follows: *If the Great Spirit did not wish you to have the privilege of sharing creation, and by so doing expressing your latent divinity, there would be no point in your being born. That is the balance that you must strike, whether you so expand your character that you choose to develop the latent gifts that you have in service that enables them to burgeon.*

So – What are we saying? You cannot focus only on one aspect of your being for example your career (mind and intellectual activities), or your body (exercise, diet and nutrition) or on spiritual matters (religion, spirituality and philosophies). You have to develop all of them simultaneously to have perfect balance in your life and to grow your soul.

You have to live your fullest life; a life in which all your talents, faculties and gifts find their fullest manifestation. By doing this, you will serve the purpose of your earthly being (your individual purpose in life) and you will be ready for the next stage of your life when the door of death opens to you. Equipped you can now enter the spiritual plane and prepare for the next level.

The whole purpose of your earthly life is that you live on all aspects of your being. You need to sustain balance- spiritually, mentally, and physically.

Chapter 3

Who Are You?

The real you is the spirit – the soul, the divine, the eternal.

Are you aware of the true you? You have to make a major paradigm shift within your own thinking and be aware of the greatness within you – you are a tiny fraction of God.

One of life's biggest misconceptions is that you have a physical body with a spirit. Even though you believe that you have a soul or a spirit, you think about yourself as a body with a spirit. This is incorrect. The truth is that you are a *spirit* with a body.

When you say that you would like to find out which is you and which is not you, you have to begin by discovering which is you altogether. When you think of you as the whole self – the consciousness – what do you think?

You as you think about you, mirror or reflects only a fraction of the greater, complete consciousness, which is the *real you*. The real you is the spirit – the soul, the divine, the eternal.

You are a spiritual being and not a body of substance alone. The body is the house in which you live. You are the tenant. The body is only the house - it is not *you*. You have to maintain and keep the house in a good condition. You have to repair the house to be able to look after the tenant sufficiently. You are a spiritual being expressing yourself through the physical body and the spirit is the supreme part of you. The body is the flesh and blood. Your body is made up of the muscle and the skin thus, the body is not you. The body is the lower - the spirit is the higher. The body is the servant - the spirit is the master. The body is the subject and the spirit is the king. The part of you, which is divine, is your spirit. The body is fashioned to only serve its purpose and that is to host your incarnated spirit. The body is temporary in its existing form. The body crumbles away when it has done its task. The spirit, which has incarnated at birth and is the power of life itself, moves on to the spiritual plane because your spirit is infinite.

When you accept this knowledge it means your soul is ready; it has come into its own. The fact that you read this book and that you are able to receive this knowledge means that the divine has awakened within you, and your spiritual nature has come into its own.

You have reached that stage of development when you are ready to obtain from life, not that which exists only on the surface, but all the riches that belongs only to the spirit. You are ready to embrace and engage the energies from Source that will take you to another level of consciousness. You are aware that you are a Special Being from the Light.

Chapter 4

What is The Spirit?

The spirit which breathed life into us, has given us a common link, because throughout the whole world all the children of the Great Spirit are fundamentally united. The spirit that enables them to live on earth and beyond is the same spirit that makes them a vast family with a common, divine parent.

S. Birch

An Infinite Supreme Divine Being

You have to understand that Spirit is infinite and that it is very difficult to give a complete picture of Spirit. Words are finite and even with my best attempt to explain the Spirit I will still lack to describe the fundamental and inherent power, which I am trying to describe. I can only aspire to explain Spirit as I experience Spirit and understand Spirit with my limited knowledge and level of my own soul-growth at this stage to the best of my ability.

Spirit is the power, which is life itself. Without Spirit, there is no life, for life is Spirit and Spirit is life. Spirit is the primal substance of ALL life. Spirit embraces the most miniature and the most majestic. The association or relationship of Spirit is the common nexus and link in all life. It means that Spirit is the interconnection or bond to all life. Spirit is the fountainhead, which gives life from microscopic level on earth to the angelic and higher planes beyond. Spirit is the origin of all existence. Spirit is the starting point meaning the beginning and the end. Think of the phrase *I AM THAT I AM* when God had a conversation with Moses at the burning bush: Exodus 3.14. Think of God as the life and breath of the whole universe. Look around you and when you experience God's beauty of creation, you will know that you are fortunate and truly blessed to be a particle of this Infinite Supreme Divine Being. God is the highest ultimate power!

We all know that God is not a personal, cruel, dictatorial, tyrannical, vengeful being. God is the perfect Law and the Law is God. God is the mind of the law and the supreme power responsible for the life in the whole cosmos. The inescapable natural law is perfect and God is the law. God cannot operate outside His own laws. There is a framework, a pattern, and only within that framework and pattern can natural law operate. If you would like guidance and help from Spirit, you have to provide the conditions by which guidance and help can come to you.

You have, because you are spiritual beings, all the dormant and hidden power of God within you. Spirit is infinite, and you have an interconnection with this infinite Spirit. In miniature, in microcosm you have the great powers that belong to God. Consciousness is individual life, which is Spirit. The inspiring truth is that man is an expression of consciousness, and consciousness is the all-important thing. *You are the Great Spirit and the Great Spirit is you. S. Birch*

By understanding and accepting the truth that you are God in miniature, you will be able to realize that the kingdom of heaven is within you. By realizing this, you will automatically express your spirit through virtues such as acts of goodness, kindness, sympathy, toleration, mercy, friendship, love, compassion and affection.

The more good you do, will result in manifestation of a greater spirit, and you will advance your soul- growth. It is through the soul that the Creator and the individual connect or unite. By uniting with Spirit, you can always draw on this invisible wellspring.

What is the difference between spirit, soul and conscience?

In the soul of human beings at their best there is an unconquerable spirit. Paul S Mcelroy

Dictionaries, books, dogmas, teachings, The Bible and various religions have contradicting views on spirit and soul. Through various studies, research and searching within myself for truth and understanding of one's spirit and soul, I have come to the following understanding through trusting the guidance from above and from within:

Spirit

Spirit is God, which is life. Spirit is the supreme energy of all life. Your spirit is the life force and the breath of life itself. This means that spirit is within the immortal soul, which is the consciousness. Spirit gives the soul its life and its consciousness.

In John 4.24 we read that God is a spirit. The spirit is that part of the Creator which we call God and which expresses itself through us. Spirit is the part of us, which has a divine longing to unfold higher and higher. Spirit (God) expresses itself through successive instruments (us) as it evolves higher and higher. We have no knowledge of spirit apart from its expression, for until the spirit expresses itself we do not know it. When you unfold that which is of the spirit you expand soul-growth.

Soul

The soul is the center (headquarters) of consciousness, which differentiates between right and wrong. You cannot cut your body open to find the soul because there is no part of the body where the soul dwells. The soul fills all space and it is consciousness. I believe that the *soul* and the *conscience* work hand in hand thus: *Conscience* is that part of the soul, which tells the difference between right and wrong. Conscience is the pointer of the soul. The soul is the Creator within which is the seat of real live, the vitality or psyche. The psyche is one's mind, consciousness and awareness. When you unfold your soul you develop your psychic faculty.

We have a physical body and a spiritual body. Our body gives vibrations, which results into the state of the body. We can diagnose the health of an individual through monitoring his physical body and his state of mind. When someone is mentally not well the state of the individual's soul will be out of balance.

One of the explanations in the Webster describes soul as *a man's moral and emotional nature as distinguished from his mind or intellect (a spiritual or moral force).* In 1 Thessalonians 5.23 it says, *I pray God your whole spirit and soul...*Soul is the total self, which expresses wholeness through spirit. The real you is the spirit, which is locked within your soul and is the energy that is greater than any energy known on earth. This energy is spirit, which gives you life. When you accept and understand this knowledge you allow the spirit to manifest in your life and your soul to awaken to the realities of life.

Chapter 5

The Infinite Cycle of Life

Seeing patterns in creation is fundamental to recognizing one's individual purpose in life.
D. Krafchow

You have to learn how to interpret the physical world through spiritual understanding and through the infinite cycles of life. The Cabala (tree of life) teaches us that humanity is the mouth peace between heaven and earth and that the purpose of man is to bring light down to earth. Silver Birch teaches us to be Lightworkers. *Bring comfort or light to one who is struggling in darkness. Seek only truth, knowledge and wisdom. If you can help one soul to find itself, you have justified your existence.* S. Birch

Speech is a form of action; as the Bible says, *God spoke the world into being.* The utterance of God's name YHVH created the world. Creation is a language of rules of communication between our Creator and the creation known as the inescapable natural laws of nature, which is cause and effect. God interacts with us through the rules (natural law) of creation – what you sow you will reap. God speaks to you through the natural law of cause and effect. Keep in mind that God is the law as we discussed in the previous chapter. You, through your actions determine your fate; you register your own spiritual growth. You are who you are.

Equate your human life to the seasonal cycles of nature. These seasonal cycles control your life. Spring is the greatest season of all for this is when birth came to our world. Every human life repeats the seasonal cycle; and every human soul duplicates the display of nature. First there is the spring, when your

23

consciousness awakens; then the summer blooms, when your powers rise to their highest; then autumn follows, when your life begins to fade; and then winter follows, when sleep comes to your worn out, tired soul.

After the winter of the physical world, you go into a new cycle of rebirth. Spring comes and your spirit awakens in another world to continue the eternal cycle. Take from nature this inspiring message, and be assured that God's natural laws will never fail you. By understanding that you are a spiritual being and linked to Infinite Spirit you will realize that the cycles of life are ongoing and everlasting.

Chapter 6

The Seven Year Cycles of Human Life

We see that the cycles of life really constitute a geometrical map or a mathematical scheme whereby we can mechanically and accurately map out our lives and the external influences, and either take advantage of these things, or innocently & ignorantly submit to them. In the one case we are masters of our destiny, and in the other case victims of our fate.

H Spencer Lewis-1929

According to the primary cycle of the ancients, human life is divided into a progression of periods, each period lasting approximately seven complete sun years or seven years of approximately 365 days each. We can divide our lives into periods of seven years and we will be able to trace back

The Seven Year Cycles of Human Life

Spring	Summer	Autumn	Winter
#1 Period 1 - 7 Y	**#4 Period 21 - 28 Y**	**#7 Period 42 - 49 Y**	**#10 Period 63 - 70 Y**
Babyhood – Early Youth. Mental and Self-Discovery Physical Body Control, Fundamental Education, Relate to Material World Relate to Cultural World	Strong Development in Emotional Nature and All Psychic Faculties -- Intuition, Telepathy, Clairvoyance, etc. Growing interest in art and religious beliefs.	Desire to Rest, Meditate and Philosophically Speculate Forms New Character. New Person with New Hopes, Desires, Passion, Goal and Ideal for which to Labor. Mind on Spirit and Service	Evolves to Highly Attuned Spirituality, Progressive Evolvement to a Living Soul Approaching Inevitable Purpose of Soul Growth. Finding Spirit Within.
#2 Period 7 - 14 Y	**#5 Period 28 - 35 Y**	**#8 Period 49 - 56 Y**	**#11 Period 70 - 77 Y**
Important Physical Changes in Male and Female - Gender Aware Secondary Changes in Mental Side of Nature	Creative Processes of Mind Most Active. Strong Ability to Imagine and Mentally Create. Attunement with Cosmic Consciousness and Ethical Standards of Life. World-wide Aspirations.	Migration from the physical being to Spiritual Being. Retires from Personal Ambition with Slow Reduction in Physical Vitality – Compensated by Highly Attuned Spirituality.	Highly Attuned Spirituality. A Living Soul in Total Peace and Harmony with the World. Enlightened within. Sharing Experience and Wisdom to the World.
#3 Period 14 - 21 Y	**#6 Period 35 - 42 Y**	**#9 Period 56 - 63 Y**	**#12 Period 77 - 84+ Y**
Primary Development of Psychic side of Human Nature. Individual Character, Responsibility. Capability and Legal Accountability Established	Desire to Explore and Reveal Great Knowledge and Hidden Facts of Life. Restlessness Comes into Nature. Move Away from Selfishness. Service to Humanity. Sharing Insight Benefits with Masses.	Continuation of Spirituality. Mellowing of Mental Faculties and Physical Progress. In Harmony with the Entire Purpose of the Life Cycle of Progression.	Understands the Universal Rhythm of Life and the Inescapable Natural Cosmic Laws. Virtuous Living Secures Spiritual Rewards.

how each period has brought its definite results or produced effects upon our development, personal growth, and our mastership.

You have to keep in mind that these basic cycles are only indicators to assist you. The manifestations in each individual's life are in accordance with his or her stage of evolutionary development.

Chapter 7

Your Continuous Life's Journey

What you express on earth is only a tiny fraction of the individuality to which you belong. You belong to a 'group soul' a single unity with facets, which have spiritual relationships that incarnate at different times, at different places, for the purpose of equipping the larger soul for its work.

S. Birch

To understand your continuous life's journey you have to think about your life as a labyrinth. The essential symbolic meaning of the labyrinth will give you understanding in the stages to your life experiences. Experience the stages of the wellness wheel as the roadmap of your soul. Each stage has its own structure, strength, and contains an archetype, a message of life. This model moulds you to your soul's evolution and eventually soul-growth. The soul only learns and grows through life experience. Each experience is unique, keep in mind that all experiences are linked to one another. Your incarnated soul, as you, the spiritual being, plays the part of intermediary or mediator. You are the incarnation of a spiritual being whose destiny is to never become fixed but to constantly transform from one state to another. As a spiritual being, you are destined to evolve. You draw your progressive strength, vitality, enthusiasm and your dynamism from your weaknesses and your limitations. Only through challenges and experiences, can the soul develop and advance. You eternally (without end) go from one stage to another and, in this way, you follow your life path on the road of advancement, leaving one experience to thrust into another. Death is one of the experiences, but it is only a stage, an experience amongst so many others, not an end in itself but rebirth. This stage and learning experience is not at the beginning or at the end of your life, but in the centre and ongoing. No part of your journey, no experience is an end in itself; it is only stages of life during your journey. We are the ones wishing that our life *all this that we have now* would last forever. We are the ones wanting to fix ourselves in one particular state, which is a self-imposed illusion. All that ties us to this material physical world is what we have tied ourselves to. When we for one moment, identify ourselves as a *Spiritual Being* as *The Self*, and enter the spiritual wellness wheel of life, we will understand the essential symbolic meaning of the labyrinth of life. Then you will be conscious of your limitations and yet you will know your strengths and your powers. You will understand that life is Spirit and Spirit is eternal life.

The Infinite Spiritual Wellness Wheel

Chapter 8

The Twenty-Two States of Natural Being and Consciousness

What we do on some great occasion will probably depend on what we already are; and what we are will be the result of previous years of self-discipline.

H. P. Liddon

You are always at the entrance and the exit of the labyrinth of life - the entrance and exit of the infinite spiritual wellness wheel of life. Self-discovery is the beginning (0) but it is also completion (Twenty-Two) of life. The number 22 designates a state of existence and consciousness at the end of a completed cycle and the practical application of wisdom attained. You are already what you are trying to become. When you seek truth and are true to yourself, all your activities and actions will manifest virtue.

State One: Self-Discovery

Great men are little men expanded; great lives are ordinary lives intensified.

W. A. Peterson

You are always migrating to the unknown, inner-self. Your mind is open and highly imaginative, yet you have unrealistic ideals. You have to learn to trust on your inner guidance which is your intuition and inner wisdom, to find your way forward. You know you are on the right path, experiencing and learning what you must for your own wellness, regardless of how this may appear to others. You will find the strength for perseverance on your path and discover your truest interest and the *virtues* of life through self-examination of your inner strength and faith.

Truth comes to you when you seek with simplicity and honesty, like a little child to find your truth no matter how great the sacrifice. The ultimate truth is that you are a fragment of God living in a human body.

The *self-discovery process* helps you to test truth through instinct and reason. Instinct and reason are the great guides on our life path. We are equipped to think rationally (with our mind) and intuitively (with our heart) before we reach any decision.

As a spiritual being, you know everything, but you are unaware of your wisdom. You have to submit yourself to the numerous trials of life to develop all your faculties and become the enlightened being that you potentially are. Your mind steps into the unknown- the inner self. You are looking ahead at a distant goal and you have the wisdom that higher forces are protecting you. Your soul has an inner motivation to grow and to question the nature of reality. You have to expand your mind through internal vision, trusting and following your own inner guidance. You possess true wisdom, which makes you at times wiser than those around you. You see instinctively what even the wise cannot see, but you are unaware of this wisdom within you. You are wise enough to know that you have to purify your soul by releasing the things in life, which keep you in bondage to your lesser self, and impede your soul- growth.

By stepping into the unknown you meet up with many obstacles, overcome many trials, suffer many temptations, fulfill other tasks, play at being a hero, get married, have a family, etcetera and completely forget the object and reason for your journey. Circumstances and responsibilities have diverted you from your goal. During the cosmic cycles of your life you will hear a subtle whisper from your inner voice and your will remember, and you will leave again to start the new beginning and take up your quest where you have left.

You have to develop virtue intelligences, which represent the triumph forces of love, wisdom, and power, and the aspiration toward unity with Spirit. Well-developed virtue intelligences will allow you to take full advantage of your strength and skill intelligences in realizing your passion. Therefore, you have to be born over again, and start life all over again. You have to experience one state after another, until you understand the part that you have to play, and discover who you really are. You will see that each state of life will ask questions and that you have to do personal introspection. Each stage will confront you with a mystery (enigma) which will coincide with a human experience and will result in a new awareness. Through self-discovery, you will have the wisdom that you have to be bold enough to set off exploring to the next state of life. You will act with truth and integrity in all of your endeavors through the wisdom you have gained. By being bold in finding yourself, you will awaken your will power.

State Two: Willpower-Awakening

Strength does not come from physical capacity. It comes from indomitable will.
J. Nehru

When you experience an encounter with your willpower, you are trying to find yourself. Your willpower is that part of you that inaugurates self-transformation. Willpower means that you are perfecting yourself through transcending *the self* through the possession and exercise of your creative powers. We need to find the inner magic within ourselves. Without some inner magic, our real self will lie forever hidden under the confused world of emotions, physical needs and conditioning.

During this state of your existence, you have to acquire and experience the meaning of your existence, the meaning of love, the meaning of wisdom and the meaning of your inner realization. You are ready to take risks through your strength of will and your self-confidence. Choose to be similar to a sage who exerts the power of his will over the physical world of nature and life. Never be confused by the reality of your circumstances and things around you. Search for the magic, which is within you. This magic within is the pure product of your will, mind and heart. Realize that you yourself give magic to the world through the power of your will, which has an effect on humanity and your environment. By exercising your willpower, you will gain the application of spiritual knowledge; you will use your mental powers to overcome obstacles, you will understand the emotional plane, and you will be able to accomplish your tasks on the material physical plane. Through applying your inner magic you will be able to master the four planes of the physical world (physical or material plane, spiritual plane, emotional plane and mental plane) and you will be able to deal with any life situation.

The whole purpose of your earthly life is to live on all aspects of your being, emotionally, spiritually, mentally, and physically. You are not fulfilling yourself until these four are functioning in harmony. By connecting the spiritual to the physical through your willpower, you learn to establish concert, rhythm, harmony, balance and wholeness between your spirit, mind and body. You are able to master your soul, thoughts, and emotions and to take action. Through mastering your will, you are wise, skillful, confident, and have initiative and willpower. You translate ideas into actions, deal with difficulties, and control and direct your life. You have the ability to master and apply your psychic abilities and spiritual gifts for honorable service to humanity. You cannot have knowledge without the responsibility that knowledge brings. The wise person mixes elements according to the wisdom of the heart to produce the miraculous.

State Three: Dedication and Goals - Set a Life Goal Based on Truth

The person who makes success of living is the one who sees his goal steadily and aims for it unswervingly. That is dedication.
C. B. DeMille

You can only enter the next state of the developmental journey of your life by personifying understanding, which gives birth to knowing. You acquire knowing through soul-growth and spiritual attainment. You have to develop your psychic faculty and spiritual gifts through intuitive insight, creative ability and the revelation of hidden things. You have to learn to listen to your inner voice.

Certainty comes only from within. When your soul is ready it knows – that is the only assurance that matters. Knowledge is not fixed, but certainty is the inner realization that you at last have come face to face with truth.

You have to open the bridge between heaven and earth to help you find truth in your beliefs. You only find truth when you free your mind of all misconceptions and prejudices instilled by your upbringing and errors of the past. We experience truth when we become like little children and liberated to find our truths. It is through simplicity that you learn truth. When you learn to listen to the subtle whispers of your inner voice it will result into manifestation and understanding truth. No knowledge alters truth. There is no wisdom that in any way alters the truth of any teaching. If it was true in the past, it is true today and it will be true tomorrow. Truth is constant and eternal. You can add to wisdom, you can add to knowledge, but you cannot bring new truth.

Reach beyond your grasp. Your goals should be grand enough to get the best of you.
P. T de Chardin

You have to use your will properly so that you can be able to act on your will and bear fruit. When you leave your will to its own devices it will be scattered or wasted. A fruitless will is barren, unproductive, unreal and empty of all meaning. You have to mould your will into a distinct shape, and have its power channeled so that your will may give the best of itself. Your will needs a goal. We set our own boundaries in life by measuring, weighing up, evaluating, estimating and categorizing. Set a life goal based on truth. Your physical world has all the truth that it requires for its essential purpose. These fundamental truths are kindness, service and love. Dedicate your goals to these truths. When you set a goal, you have a purpose, outcome or resting place for your activities and actions to manifest. You have to now focus your will on what it is that you want in relation to your life or current circumstances. When you fix your mind on something, then this thing (goal) exists. The more knowledge you have the less choice you have. Increasing knowledge precisely dictates the part that you must play. You have to play your part through dedication until your mission is accomplished. The individual, who acts wisely or exerts his will in a wise manner, has overcome the second obstacle of foolishness and ignorance. Now you can go on to the next state of your life's journey.

State Four: Manifestation - Insight and Fertility

Always do the best. What you plant now, you will harvest later.
O. Mandino

Manifestation is the act of bringing something from thought to physical matter. You need desires, dreams, thoughts, ideas and seeds for manifestation. Your desires create visions and visions create your manifestations. In this state of your life, you have to awaken your conscious mind through acquiring insight. To tap into your inner vision you have to be able *to read between the lines.*

First understand consciousness. You are an expression of

consciousness, which is the key. Consciousness is individual life and the most important part of you being. Wherever there is consciousness, there is individual spirit. When you think about your soul, you cannot think of the soul as within or without. The soul fills all space. It is your consciousness. The limitations of the body cannot affect your soul. Your soul can range throughout all infinity, reaching to its heights of evolution. Consciousness is that part of you which is the fragment of God which lives inside your human body.

When your will is fruitful you can manifest joy and use it properly. Your manifestations begin as an idea or a seed, which meets with a feeling and when you nurture and love your idea, it manifests. Choose carefully that which you wish to manifest. When your conscious mind unites matter and spirit you have become conscious of the mighty power that is part of you. Through your new insight, you will now not be confused and focus on the temporary joys of earth, but on the enduring things of the spirit. Through your fertile thoughts, you will focus on spiritual matters. Insight results into knowing that all the things of matter will fade away. Ambitions, desire, the acquisition of wealth, all these are of no account. You will have the inner knowing that you will remain a spiritual being, and that your riches will be just what is contained within your own nature, no more and no less. Once you learn this, you are wise because you have found yourself and, having found yourself, you will have found God.

New insight will guide you to act with joy and will teach you that the spirit manifests through kindness, tolerance, sympathy, love, service and the doing of good works to all of creation. By trusting your inner vision, you are aware that only you are the gardener of your soul. God has provided you with everything necessary for your soul to grow in understanding, wisdom, elegance, grace and magnificence. You have to experience this truth, and then you are ready to manifest joy in all of your actions. Be willing to put the energy, effort and drive into your manifestations. Know what you want and why you want it and then visualize having it in your life. Always work for the good of those around you. Guard your intentions and trust that the universe has abundance for everyone. With your new insight, you will know that manifestations come to those who believe and trust they deserve it. You will also now focus on spiritual manifestations such as receiving inspiration, wisdom, truth, knowledge and service to God and humanity. You are ready to experience the next state of consciousness.

State Five: Vision - Sight-Power of Action

Other people may not have had high expectations for me, but I had high expectations for myself.
S. Miller

When you focus on a vision, you create the mental landscape for your life goals. During this state of your consciousness, your intellectual mind provides you with the skill and creative ability to create pictures of the future you desire. To visualize something is to *see* it in your mind; you make it visible in your mind. The power of your mind is enormous and through your mind-power, you can tap into this intelligence. By personifying your sight, you will be able to change and achieve whatever you focus on through creative visualization. Your life will be what you imagine it to be when you focus on your vision. Your mental images are living pictures with magnetism. They attract what you are dreaming of into your life. When you have a clear vision and you open your third eye to receive divine guidance, you will manifest God's blessings in your life through your visualizations, thoughts and your actions.

True vision reveals God's divine plan for all things. Through the power of visualization, you will receive the valuable benefit of imagination and attracting blessings into your life. A clear vision will assist you to balance your thoughts between uncon-sciousness, awareness and illusion. Create new positive visions through visualization and attract whatever your heart desires. Move forward with great confidence and with the knowledge that all the forces of goodness, helpfulness and service are at your side. Use your innate powers of imagination and manifestation. Imagination recharges you with the power of God and assists you to inspire, guide, uphold and sustain a positive mindset. Fill your conscious mind with divine wisdom, which will provide you with the visualization skills, the capacity to understand and receive visions, and the ability to be able to move forward.

When you have a clear vision, you will have the ability to use mental control over emotions and the ability to successfully execute plans of action. Your actions will be mature, intelligent, experienced, confident and reasonable. You will be able to find contracts, clients, customers, careers, hobbies, people and all that you desire. Through visualization, you can manifest spiritual, mental and material freedom. The truth is that you can manifest whatever you desire through the realization that God is within you. Use this knowledge as a powerful visualization tool to attract God's blessings into your life.

State Six: Search - Intuitive Knowing
You can always find the sun within yourself if you will only search.
M. Maltz

I have learned we hear with our hearts, not our ears, we understand with our intuition, not our minds.
P. Rodegast, *Emmanuel's Book.*

During this state of consciousness, your inner voice speaks to you. You have awakened your intuition. When you awaken your intuition, you become conscious. When you truly become conscious you can leverage your inner wisdom and knowledge.

You are now able to receive inspiration and inspired thoughts from your subconscious- and conscious mind.

You are searching for the secret of life. You are searching for peace with God, the world, everybody in it but most importantly, with yourself. You are searching for rhythm, harmony, balance and wholeness. Your soul has an pressing intense need to break free from the material world to the divine, to experience serenity and peace. Your intuition will assist you in accomplishing self-change.

When you awaken to the secret of life, you will have the wisdom that your mind, body and spirit are equally important. You will have the wisdom to integrate your body, mind and spirit in all your actions. You act now on your intuition and faith rather than on force or mind. You are now able to filter all your thoughts through your heart before they become actions.

The capacity to restrain your inspiration is like holding one's tongue instead of speaking one's truth. It is the small light, which illuminates the darkness. Through your intuitive knowing you are able to live and awaken to give service, upliftment and selfless love to humanity. Your spiritual awakening has emerged and you have found the expression of spirit, which lives within you. You will achieve spiritual awakening through intuition, insight and spiritual self-discipline, allowing the ego-self and trans-personal self to work in harmony and unity. As you emerge into light, you will experience true happiness and peace through your spiritual awakening. You will have exciting expectations of your future. You will have hope, and joys you will have a striving towards your spiritual existence to make a difference to humanity. You are now able to move on to the next state.

State Seven: Compassion - Power of Love

The gifts I wish to give you are my deepest love, the safety of truth, the wisdom of the universe and the reality of God. Emmanuel

A warm smile is the universal language of kindness.
Anonymous

One of the oldest universal spiritual truths taught by the old masters such as Socrates, Buddha, Jesus and Silver Birch is that love governs all communication. Love is the key. Love is the greatest force and source of energy. Love works wonders that no other power can achieve. Love desires no ill will for any person or any living thing. 1 Corinthians 13 teaches us all the attributes of love, verse 13 *And now abideth faith, hope, charity/love, these three; but the greatest of these is charity/love.*

You have to awaken your consciousness and feelings of eternal selflessness and unconditional love and compassion. God's unconditional love is the only love, which satisfies the need of the soul. Selfless love denies the self which means giving without expecting anything in return.

The unconditional love of God is the strongest force in the universe. It surrounds loving partnerships, motherhood, marriage, friendship and love for the whole universe and all of the creation. Your soul has an urge to connect with God. To obtain the best results in connecting with God there must be an attraction between the two worlds and the highest attracting force is the power of love. Love calling to love is the reason why all the barriers between 'heaven' the spiritual plane and earth, the physical plane, get broken down. You must have an overwhelming desire to connect and to be of service to your Creator. The virtue of your desire will ensure that God's love fulfills you. God is perfect love and perfect wisdom. God is life and love, and He fills all life. He is everything. You should have the desire to connect with your Creator and to experience this unconditional love. The Father desires your desire for Him. Why does He desire your love? He wants you to stimulate the divine within you and to help you to unfold your spirit. Love is the basis of His desire. He loves you and you are His child by your dormant divinity. You show your love to God by acknowledging that He is a part of you. You want to fulfill your purpose of your being. The love is the incentive from the Creator for you to stimulate your spirit and through demonstrating the power of love, the spirit should have found itself. You are now on your path at the beginning of your spiritual development. You have to develop your spirit so that your spirit can be ripe for the next stage of your existence. 1 Corinthians 13.7 reminds us that Love is the Golden Thread of Life!

Find compassion in your heart through unconditional selfless love towards humanity. Compassion is a deep feeling for and understanding of misery or suffering and the simultaneous desire to promote its improvement. When you practice compassion, you have a spiritual consciousness of the personal tragedy of another or others and selfless tenderness directed towards it. You have to touch souls and do work that will lift the sorrows of others and make their lives better. When you really want to make a difference you have to bring light where there is darkness. By practicing compassion you can raise up those who have fallen down, give strength to individuals who are week, give food to those who are hungry and sleep to those who have nowhere else to go. When you are a compassionate instrument for God, you are ready to experience the next state. The seal of divine approval is a certainty when you act with compassion and love towards all of creation.

The real man is the one who strives to uplift his fellows, who sees only a wrong to be righted, barriers to be crushed, ignorance to be driven out, hunger to be abolished, and slams that which must be uprooted. These are God's spiritual truths. S. Birch

State Eight: Effort - Victory - Mastery of Selfishness

It's not necessarily the amount of time you spend at practice that counts; it's what you put into the practice.
E. Lindros

In this state of consciousness, you have to learn how to harness the power of the wild beast, which is within us all. Our wild untamed beast is that part of us that kindles selfishness and materialism. When your actions are self-centered and selfish, the consequences eventually end up in misery, tears, chaos, confusion and disaster. This wild untamed beast is that part of your soul which responds to lower vibrations. You can choose to unfold your soul and you can choose to unfold your spirit. One is the development of only the psychic faculty, and the other is soul-growth. When you choose to only develop your psychic faculty without spiritual development, you have a lower plane of vibration. You should be dissatisfied when you act on this vibration. Intuitively you experience dissatisfaction and you struggle towards greater freedom. If you are satisfied, you stagnate. When you do that which is not right, inside your heart you know it is not right. Whether you resist it or not, depends on the character which you have grown for yourself. You have to control all your thoughts and actions. All deeds of selfishness are sin. Whether you sin with the body, mind or the spirit, all is sin. It means that you act on impulse or desire, which comes from your thoughts. You are like an instrument, which receives thoughts and sends out thoughts, but the thoughts that you receive depend upon your character and your spirit. You have to evolve your soul and strive for progress. Your desires attract those vibrations with similar desires. When you do not harness the wild untamed beast, you act selfishly.

You need to overpower powerful thoughts of selfishness through your free will. This takes enormous effort. When you have not mastered the wild untamed beast those who face you face a formidable challenge. Effort is required for you in order to improve or resolve your state of mind to accomplish victory. By understanding opposing forces, you can control and direct your nature. You have to be willing to do what is needed and you have to be active and persevere rather than taking the easy option.

When you have a clear purpose or objective, then you can become constructive and harness the forces of the physical world into balance and harmony. When you grow your soul and you are doing what is right for you, then the effort required becomes a pleasure. Your efforts will be more productive if they are of an overall healthy balanced life. There is nothing like the rewards of energy well spent, and when your efforts result in progress forward and advancing your soul-growth. Soul-growth is the spiritual victory! It is better to be tested and to win than not to be tested and thus be unaware of your undeveloped strengths and power within. You have to put in the effort to learn, and by learning, you will grow, evolve, advance, develop, unfold and go forward. You have to take it slowly and you have to remember that to accomplish the rewards of spirit requires careful cultivation, nurturing and progress. Sudden conversions would not be enduring, and your effort must be towards permanent self-mastery. With continuous effort, you can combine your psychic- and spiritual development and become a great individual. You will gain victory by counteracting selfishness and becoming profound and well balanced. Self-control, personal effort and perseverance will take you into the next state of learning.

State Nine: Integrity - Boundaries of Conduct

Excellence implies more than competence – it implies a striving for the highest possible standards.
Anonymous

The Webster Dictionary defines integrity as an uncompromising adherence to a code of moral, artistic, or other values. When you have integrity, you are utterly sincere, honest and truthful. You avoid deception, expediency, artificiality or shallowness of any kind. You always act ethically with no exception. It means that your state of being is undivided and complete. You have accomplished material, spiritual, or aesthetic wholeness.

Knowing the difference between true and false, and to maintain integrity is a profound act. Our logic and inner voice determine what we believe is right. You have to weigh the value of all things and maintain a balance between outer and inner harmony. You achieve this through intentions filled with integrity and by being an honest person who is responsible for his or her own decisions and actions.

Integrity means that you will set boundaries and honor them in all of your actions. You have to attune yourself to the natural laws of cause and effect. What you sow, you will reap. You are on earth to build your character and you can only grow by choosing to always do the right thing. You cannot be a great soul by achieving results easily. You have to make choices in your life for example: If you choose to live selfishly you must reap the results of selfishness. When you choose to be intolerant, prejudiced or unfair you will reap the results of intolerance, prejudice and unfairness. The natural law is unalterable and the law is unchallengeable. The effect always follows cause with methodical and mechanical certainty.

To hold a boundary you have to get clear and consistent. Always let people know about your boundaries and be willing to take action if they do not respect them. Boundaries are about self-control and self-respect. If you do what you know is right, then you cannot do any more. If that means that sometimes you must deny yourself, then you must do it.

Boundaries are also about respecting others. It is easy to push others and manipulate them into giving us what we want. When you do this, there is always a price to pay. Choose to act right; you may need to look at how you fail to respect boundaries of others.

Having and keeping to your own boundaries takes commitment and discipline. It is about restricting yourself appropriately. Go ahead and discover how wonderful it feels to be in charge of yourself and to manifest powerful opportunities through your acts of integrity. When you desire the growth of your spirit, you must live that kind of live which alone can assure spiritual growth. The spirit grows through acts of integrity, kindness, compassion, love, sympathy, fairness and service. When your actions portray integrity, you have mastered one of the greatest virtues of life. Through your free will, you have chosen to awaken your consciousness to grow your spirit.

State Ten: Aspiration - Consciousness Discovered

You will become as small as your controlling desire; as great as your dominant aspiration.
J. Allen

State ten, represents finding new beginnings through your God-consciousness and sharing this knowledge with others. Your soul is now on its way to rebirth and will begin to find expression. You are now wiser and the soul that knows - has self-control, calmness and resolution. You know with certainty that the power, which gives life, which rules the universe, which makes provision for all that breathes and moves, cannot fail you. This power guides you and is your compass throughout your life's journey. This inner guidance is an ongoing process where you not only set off in the right direction, but also monitor the journey as you travel.

With the new inner wisdom that you have gained, you are aware that the spiritual quest is a lonely quest, and that your life will follow your aspirations. You are now aware that the smallest light illuminates the darkness. You have to aspire to guide others. Guidance involves instruction and influence of a more subtle nature. The small light illuminates, the flashlight blinds. At this state of consciousness, you aspire to be a Lightworker. You are also aware that you should not fail your Creator, so that your actions never betray the trust that rests in you, what you are receiving and for the wisdom that you have acquired. Your now have a responsibility to share your wisdom and knowledge with the rest of the world. You must be willing to follow through on sharing spiritual truths.

Always aspire to master your energy, thoughts, desires and actions on an ongoing basis. You are aware that progress is eternal and that you cannot see the whole picture at this moment. You have to aspire and persevere in your quest for soul-growth, and you have to search consistently for enlightenment. You have to find your real self, the inner truth through meditation and contemplation. Now is also the time to look for guidance from within. Trust your intuition. You have wisdom that everything is in accordance with divine law, divine love, divine wisdom and divine justice.

Consciousness produces thoughtful action that is no longer free but responsible, clear-minded and conscious of course. You always have to act with care, thoughtfulness and respect, be trust-worthy and willing to account for your actions. Create some space to hear what your own advice is and then take it. You receive opportunities, which can better your life and grow your soul daily. When you withdraw from the outer world and meditate, you are inspired to receive new thoughts and visions to broaden and grow your consciousness.

You cannot have instant soul-growth. Our physical world is always anxious for short cuts to everything. It is a certainty that there are no short cuts to spiritual attainment. Soul-growth is necessarily slow, but it is sure. Your soul cannot grow and achieve its next stage of development until it is ready to do so. At this state of consciousness, you are aware that you are on the right road. Aspiration to find your God-consciousness and to share it with the world is all that matters.

State Eleven: Success - Knowledge of Destiny
Success is the maximum utilization of the ability you have.
Z. Ziglar

What we call good and bad are only stages on the road of our lives. Good and bad outline the progress and movement during our journey. Each time we return to a point we are potentially richer for having experienced the full transformation of this state, which represents our instincts, intelligence and spiritual knowledge. Through experience of all the states of consciousness and the labyrinth of life, we acquire new wisdom and receive truth, we give birth to our future and we are able to hear the subtle speech of our Creator. Truths do not change. Our minds change, but *Truth* is constant. We base *Truth* upon knowledge, and knowledge comes from God. He is the center and the source of all inspiration.

We now have the wisdom that Shekinah (the Infinite Godly Presence) soars over us like a bird over her offspring; Shekinah feels our pain and our joy as the Infinite Spiritual Presence quietly accompanies us through the years of our life. God has made provision for every facet of life. There are certain things that happen in our life which have the enduring print of the Creator. These experiences might be positive in nature or detrimental, but you know where they came from and who sent them.Whatever seed you plant, what will grow is contained within it; it will be true to its nature. Awakening only comes when realization dawns. With this new knowledge, your have awakened your spirit. Through God's laws nothing is forgotten, overlooked or neglected.

Now you can achieve whatever you desire and you are bold, brave and trusting around receiving. You believe in yourself. You now have the wisdom that your basic needs to survive will be provided for. Once you have adjusted yourself to the laws of eternal supply, you will never be hungry, or thirsty or in need of anything. You are aware that all inspiration, all wisdom, all truth, all knowledge is dependent upon your capacity to receive. You are in charge of your destiny meaning, you have power over success and failure. Through perfect faith and by living the right life you are able to attract rewards and gifts. You are confident, the more you have, the more you gain, because confidence brings success and success brings more confidence. The happier you are in your soul, the nearer you are to your Creator. All your actions portray the natural law of cause and effect. You live in harmony with the natural law and you choose to attract good vibrations. When you move on to the next stage of life (when you die) you take into the spiritual world what you are. Not what you think you are, and not what you try to show other people you are. It is what you are *inside*. You are who you are. At this state of consciousness you are aware of this spiritual truth and that this state represents the cycle of growth, perpetual change, destiny, karma; and the need for finding your centre of calmness. You are aware that the soul of every individual registers permanently all the results of his/her earthly life. You think now before you act.

Success to you is now not material but spiritual. Success is to fill your heart with love, your mind with knowledge and your spirit with a determination to serve. Success to you at this moment means that you want to spread the light further. You want to help to stop pain, misery and suffering. You want to bring happiness, peace and comfort to others. You are now confident that you are preparing your soul for its next experience when you move on beyond death.

State Twelve: Courage / Internal Strength

Courage to start and willingness to keep at it are the requisites for success.
A. Newton Benn

You have now learnt to balance your body, mind and spirit. Through the correct and persistent application of your inner strength and by controlling your mental powers you are aware that you can overcome adversity and that success is not external but internal knowing. Through your own free will, you have consciously begun to allow your inner self to develop. Through

Having acquired a developing spirit and consciousness you have become fertile and rich. Now you are the master of your destiny and master of all the circumstances around you. You are aware that your mind is the director of your intelligence and the controller of your individual life. You have the choice to actively and energetically take part in the outer materialistic world in order to mould it according to your desires; or the choice to adopt a receptive, gentle and understanding attitude, by exploring your inner strength and riches. Whatever your choose, you will not become a victim of the inescapable natural law of cause and effect, which means that the same cause produces the same effect, always, inevitably. You are now in a position where you cut yourself off from fate and become the master of your destiny. You have the inner wisdom through the riches within yourself that it is none other than the strength of love. You have now the realization that we all have an inner strength within us all, drawn from the infinite spirit world from where we came. This inner strength can calm confusion and turmoil with a smile and it can melt the most hardened heart. This awareness of the eternal, indestructible power inside us can transcend higher than any materialistic problem and its disintegration cannot affect us. You have now the courage to face any problem on your path. Courage is the power or quality, which you use when you face adversity in your life. You have the ability to be courageous through your inner strength, which is to literally tap into the God force, which is within you. Your inner strength enables you to overcome your fears and to connect with the universal energy, which surrounds and protects you. At this state of consciousness, you have mastered to obtain inner strength, courage and divine energy.

State Thirteen: Explore - Guide of the Future

If you want to succeed you should strike out on new paths rather than travel the worn paths of accepted success.
Proverbs 30.27

Now that you are the master of your destiny, you cannot live your life as you used to. You need to live your life with new motivation and in harmony with The Divine Plan of your life. You must follow your own path from creation to completion, whatever the cost. You have to be flexible, be responsive to your intuition, lose your undesirable qualities and be prepared for self-sacrifice in a good cause. You have to seek to always live a nobler life of great self-sacrifice and of optimism. Through your new wisdom, you are aware that you will not achieve that which is worth achieving without a challenge, test or some form of discomfort or distress. By going through this major life change, you have learned to turn your mind over to higher powers and to your God consciousness and have awakened to spiritual truths. You have achieved spiritual awareness by releasing your past patterns and by obtaining an alternate view of your life. You have gone through a major transition in your life and have to now readjust and explore new ideas and conditions. You have to learn now how to be free and that it will result into rejoicing in the fullness of spiritual knowledge. In this state of consciousness, you reject the personal self to attain the divine state of your mind. This state relates to the mind's union with God, and the inner peace, inspiration, and faith that results from alignment with the divine will. When we act through our heart, we act beyond logic. When your heart is superior to your head it means that chaos rules. The Cabbala teaches us that chaos paves the way to logic and is one of the higher realms. It is the chaos of light and darkness, (pleasure and will) which connects the infinite with the finite. Out of the apparent confusion, the divine pattern will take shape and harmony and peace will come. You have to explore and open your spiritual eyes to catch a glimpse of the life that you can have. You are waiting for a guide to help you, but you have to open your heart center and sense that the guidance and love needs to come from within you and not from someone else, as you stretch your arms out asking for the help and care you so want. Explore and look within *the self,* and pour the love essence with care and compassion into your heart center. The power of the spirit, which gives vision and courage, enthusiasm and desire to serve, is available daily. It is your responsibility to learn, explore and search for it through the operation of the natural laws, which will manifest blessings in your life. It will also guide you on your way forward. You are the guide you are looking for, equipped with divine reason and spiritual knowledge. You are a part of the Divine. He says to you: *Here are my laws and here, in you, is a part of Me. Besides you there is all that can be used to make a perfect universe. I give you all the tools and you can choose between the things that are right and the things that are wrong. You can try to work with My laws or against them.* At state thirteen, you have chosen to attract the vibrations of your Creator and not to follow the path of selfishness and materiality, you are now not afraid to be different and to follow your Divine Plan.

State Fourteen: Focus and Rebirth - Turning Point
Get the butterflies in your stomach to fly in formation.
B. A. Kipfer

In the previous state, you have learned to not confuse the temporary joys of the materialistic plane with the enduring things of the spirit, which symbolizes the liberation of *the self.* You have learnt to rise above your fears and your earthly problems and not to allow the vibrations of fear to hinder you. You are aware that all challenges are a necessary part of the cycle of existence. At state fourteen, you need a *symbolic death* as part of initiation for spiritual transformation. Spiritual transformation refers to the alchemical fire that transforms base forms (prime matter being black) into the superior form of pure gold. Your *symbolic death* (your old life) makes way for the new divine life, which describes the major change in your consciousness. It is only by releasing your past patterns of thinking, your personality behavior, and your lifestyle that you can open the door to manifest a better way to think and live. Death really means transformation, resurrection, the rising of the higher out of the lower. Think of the mystical bird the Phoenix, which destroys itself in the fire and rises from the ashes to become whole. You are now at a turning point in your life where you have to regenerate yourself. It is a passing between two visions of reality, one outside and the other inside. It is not a question of destruction or an end in itself and a journey of no return. It is a new exciting creation, a time of fertilization, gestation and rebirth. Through rebirth, you will enter the spring of dreams and the summer of fulfillment. You need focus and effort to improve your life from the old to the new and to be able to grow and to evolve. You can only begin to live when you symbolically *die*. The learning at this state is that you are aware that you cannot convert you life in a blinding flash like Saul on the road to Damascus. You need to continually focus and readjust yourself. There will be ongoing pitfalls. You must remember that the things of the spirit require careful fostering and you have to continuously encourage and cherish spiritual progress. A rapid conversion will not be enduring or stable. Your intentions for a new way of living and soul-growth must be permanent. You have to develop and advance your soul-growth. Always be aware that the lower cannot grasp the higher, the limited cannot include the unlimited, the lesser cannot hold the greater, but only by striving, can you increase your capacity to understand. Through focused intentions and careful nurturing, you will be able to achieve progress through focused intentions and careful nurturing. Through your ongoing focus and effort, you will be able to clarify your current and long-term objectives. Due to your ongoing focus and effort, you will be able to clarify your current and long-term objectives. By having a clear purpose you can become constructive in bringing your soul-growth to progress and with your new insight, you will help the world to advance as well. Focus and remember to look after yourself. Your rebirth process and efforts will be more productive when they are part of an overall healthy balanced life. Always harmonize your body, mind and soul; keep in mind that all the hard work is for you. Enjoy yourself and have the wisdom that when you desire to grow your spirit, you must live the kind of life, which alone can assure spiritual growth. There is nothing like the reward of your energy well spent, and when you make the attempt this will be yours along with an upturn in your spiritual growth! Focus initially involves sincere and ongoing effort and honest behavior, but when you reap the rewards, you will know that it was worth it.

State Fifteen: Skill - Patience - Revelation
It isn't by size that you win or fail – be the best of whatever you are.
D. Mallock

You have to now master the qualities of patience, endurance and creativity by directing your skills and intentions through focus and personal ongoing effort. Your focused spiritual thoughts give you the ability to find peace within you. You know that you will get results and that you are able to attract higher vibrations to help you to contemplate, to have confidence in your beliefs and to always have hope. During this state of consciousness, you learn how to use your abilities of patience and moderation in your thoughts, feelings, and actions. When you become the alchemist of your life, you are dedicated to purify the *lower self* towards transformation into the *greater self*. The symbolic death of the ego means that we strip ourselves of misconceptions, pride and the attachments and aversions we have shown towards the momentary experiences of the material life. Through the accomplishment of revelation, we are now able with the sustenance to go further. This state focuses specifically on the period that you have to learn that there are two forms of development. You have to unfold your soul and your spirit. One is the development of only the psychic faculty, and the other is soul-growth. *Where you get the development of the psychic without the spiritual, there you have a low plane of vibration. When you get a combination of both, then you have not only a great medium but a great man or woman.* S. Birch.

At this state of consciousness, you are working on developing both. Through synergy, the psychic and spiritual energies result in you being able to harness and direct your skills, intelligence, firmness, tact, and your pure intent. You are now able to use self-control, moderation, patience, and skill in dealing with all situations. You are now aware that it is through being a source of life yourself that you live. You are now like a star or a sun, which generates its own energy and its own life and light. By balancing and harmonizing the psychic and spiritual forces and applying them to your physical life you lavishly, spread your light to all around you. You have now matured as an individual and are adaptable and skillful in all of your actions. You focus now on the real important things in life meaning focusing on spiritual truth, love, trust and knowledge. Your feet are set on pathways of progress. You know that an evolved spirit cannot be afraid at any time because you know there is no experience that can come over you in any phase of your life that you cannot master, for you are a portion of God. The divine plan is perfect and you are part of it. Your responsibility is to be as pure an instrument as you can for the power of the spirit to flow through you. Be the best at whatever you are!

State Sixteen: Frugality - Resisting our Nature

You really can change the world if you care enough.
M. Wright Edelman

Strong and profound is the individual who can exercise self-control and restrain from temptation. Even after the death of the ego and the sustenance of restraint, there are dangers and difficulties. We still have to face that which is unenlightened. We have to choose between the materialistic underworld as well as the higher spiritual world, which run parallel with one another. Think of two rails on a railroad track; at all times you have the under-world and the higher world from which you can choose. When you are frugal, you are able to manage your resources carefully.

At this state of consciousness, the challenge is to look deeper within. You should have dedicated faith, which was born out of the knowledge that you have accumulated through your other states of consciousnesses. Because you are human, your mind and thoughts can still persuade you to take the path of personal power. Sometimes we are careless and vulnerable, and through temptation, our thinking and behavior results into wrong actions. We blatantly disregard the spiritual laws and its operation. Always keep in mind that you will reap what you have sown. He who sins must reap the results of his sin. Not one individual escapes his punishment for living sinfully, and not one loses his reward for living a virtuous and frugal life. When you choose to focus on the material plane and the temporary pleasures, you obscure your eternal vision and you exclude yourself from receiving higher knowledge. These pleasures are tasteless, weak, insubstantial and flimsy. The physical energy such as lust for material power and gain represent the negative powers in the psyche, the shadow in each of us, thus, it is the guardian of the threshold and the keeper of the gate to higher knowledge. It is the personification of all the hidden passions and fears within you. You have to face all these passions and fears, which you as the earnest seeker have to face within yourself before you can pass through the advanced levels of psychic and spiritual devel-opment. You are on earth to build your character and to make the right choices, which will result in soul-growth and spiritual progress. You do not need to convince your mind to live a virtuous life, influenced by frugality. Frugality mirrors the quality or state of your being, which means that you have mastered the excessive emphasis of the material world, the physical pleasures and lust for money and power. When you accomplish victory over the pitfalls and difficulty of the material world, you are able to live a life without fear, domination or bondage of any kind. You will be able to rise triumphantly over every difficulty because you are aware of the infinite power, which is within you. You have gained the wisdom that you have the power over every circumstance in your life. You can now redirect and transform your physical energy into more frugal, virtuous and spiritual pursuits.

State Seventeen: Sacrifice - Unavoidable Change

Great achievement is usually born of great sacrifice, and is never the result of selfishness.
Napoleon Hill

At this state, you have to remember that you should never forget where you came from, where you draw your essence (spirit) and strength from, where you originated from and that your life is eternal. If you persistently use your gifts wrongly and continuously make the wrong choices through your own free will, you will regress and go back to your starting point, and you may even fall lower than before.

You have to find yourself and can only do so when you feel lost and when it seems that there is no hope. You can only find a great truth through great sorrow. Positive change can come disguised as undesirable circumstances such as a sudden sickness, severe financial loss, or when someone close to you die. It is a fundamental spiritual truth that the soul begins to come into its own only when the individual has touched the lowest possible depth, when you are at your wits end and nothing material can offer even a gleam of hope. The dynamic spiritual forces have to give you a wake up call and enforce change for your soul to grow. This change is always purifying and beneficial, it helps you to cast out those remaining aspects of *the self*, which are capable of hindering your unity of being.

Suddenly *the self* is in a crisis and you experience disruption of your emotions within your body, mind and soul. You feel lost as if being trapped in a maze and you cannot find your way out. You experience feelings such as hopelessness, despair and depression.

When your life takes an unexpected turn, go with it gracefully and with trust that the divine is protecting and guiding you. When realization dawns upon you that there is nothing in the world of matter to which you can cling, it is then that your soul has its rebirth and begins to find expression. You have to sacrifice yourself in the process towards rebirth and strengthen the link that binds you to your Creator. The more you strengthen the link, the deeper becomes the channel through which help and higher power can come to you. You will receive help through a flash of inspiration and the gift of creative insight, only after self-sacrifice and when you have exhausted the pathways of your personal mind. Positive energy always reigns after a seemingly crisis. When you have victory over your crisis, you will attain your original pure and divine state of being. The soul who knows has calmness, resolution, self-control, pose and serenity. Hold on to what you know and always be steadfast. Rejoice and treasure this blessing - you are now able to face your crisis with knowledge and not with ignorance.

State Eighteen: New Beginning - Subtle Blessing
There is always a new day, a new dawn, with a new hope and a new possibility.
S. Birch

During the previous state of consciousness, you have experienced adversity and you have overcome your crisis triumphantly. You are now experiencing a new beginning and rebirth in a higher realm of your being. Your unconscious and consciousness function now as a unit and in harmony. You rely on both before making decisions. New beginnings and a sudden widening of your horizons have resulted into a new life accompanied by vigor and deep insight. In this state of being your heart is free. When you have a free heart, you do not try to enforce your influence onto someone else. With the new knowledge that you have gained, you are aware that a violent hand destroys; you now give guidance to others through a delicate hand. You live naturally and you are at one with everything around you. You do not chase abundance and are aware that through the subtle blessing of the Creator you will receive whatever you need. You place your faith in that which you have not yet seen, because you know that the laws of the universe will attract whatever you require. In life, there is kindness that is obvious, warming us with the promise of renewal. In life, there is also a kindness, which appears like a gemstone with a delicate light, which can enter the depths of our being to change the course of our life significantly. To receive this graceful blessing, you have to be prepared to gaze into the vast unknown and to follow through on your new beginning. This new beginning conveys the message of continuity and the divine purpose of your existence. It also offers faith, hope and inspiration. You will receive insight, inspiration, courage and enlightenment from your spiritual self. Through your new beginning and the subtle blessing, you will be aspired towards the state of mind whereby you will realize that the divine light dwells within you and you will see the connectedness with Spirit. You will be inspired and you will experience oneness with your Creator.

State Nineteen: Strategy - Letting Go - Meditate
By going slowly you sometimes, arrive faster.
B. A. Kipfer

You have to create your own roots through the strength of your spirit as well as your inspiration to liberate yourself. Your needs, feelings and desires tie you down, not the physical world. When you have unrealistic desires and idealistic expectations for yourself, it will result in disillusion and fear, and you will experience a deep yearning for security and fulfillment. You are now ready for the final reunion between the opposite poles of your being. Create a strategic plan for yourself on how you plan to keep a balance between the male and female, conscious and unconscious and outer and inner poles of your being. Have a focused strategy to listen to your intuition rather than reason. Rely on your divine survival kit (study figure 7 the spiritual tree of life). You have to trust yourself and listen to your inner voice to be independent. When you act through self-reliance and you have a strategy in place, you will know that it is imperative to make time for yourself to re-focus. You have to meditate to find the kingdom of heaven, which is within you. You cannot find it in the rush of the outer world. You can only find it within the silence of yourself; you will find it within your soul. It is through making yourself small, by retreating and letting go that creativity and inspiration flourishes. To go within and let it be is also a profound and powerful tool during the turmoil of life. When your energy levels are down it is your responsibility to recharge your battery. You need a strategy to withdraw for a while and to retire into the silence of your own being. Forget the world of matter with all its harsh disagreements and conflicts. Tune into the subtle, delicate vibrations of the teeming spirit life around you, and you will know that you can transcend the limitations of your fleshly body. You have to awaken to knowledge and understanding. Through your strategic choice, you have chosen not to be a hostage of this world and to leave the prison of ignorance. You uplift yourself when you withdraw for a while. Contemplate and ask questions when you have doubts. Pen down the mental thoughts that go through your mind, they are divine answers. Again, and again go over the basis of your belief and see if it will stand the test. When you find that it does, you are the better for it. When you find that it does not stand the test, then change your outlook and strategy for there is still more truth for you to acquire. Always test your answers through your reason and your intelligence. If your reason rebels and your intelligence is insulted, then disregard them. By trusting the *Divine Source*, you will grow your soul and you will live in the light of spiritual freedom.

State Twenty: Happiness - Obvious Blessing

The secret in happiness is not in doing what one likes, but in liking what one does.
J. M. Barrie

You have obtained solid roots and can now increase your growth, development and progress. During this state of consciousness and at this stage of the journey, you have established yourself as an individual in the deep, essential and absolute realities of life. Your journey is never ending and you always have to strive to reach the other levels of consciousness. Therefore, your heart is still restless, and the thoughts of the heart generate emotions. You are likely to cause emotional spirals if you are not cautious when you act on your feelings, desires and needs. You will be happy when you are in control of your emotions. Choose to direct your feelings, desires and needs towards yourself, and become one with them. Unite them with eternity, which means that you choose to have synergy between the outer worlds and inner worlds within. Full union has taken place and two have become one. When you are in control, the sense of disconnection and fragmentation at the core, your centre of the heart of human unease has disappeared. Beyond this state of consciousness that you have reached, there are other levels to cross and transverse, high above human comprehension. At this moment, you are happy and tranquil and you can savor the triumph of the spirit. When you are happy you shine, happiness is like pure light, which represents spiritual nourishment, and has the properties of kindness and warmth, and it illuminates everything in its path. When you are happy you feel renewed and your emotions are full of optimism and excitement. You have unlocked the joyous love from the correct source, which is within the core of your being, your heart center. You are poring in this love from your main artery and you are sending it out to the rest of the world. When you are happy you illuminate and inspire your mind and soul in its quest for growth and spirituality. Your vibrant and positive attitude enhances your capacity to receive inspiration, wisdom, knowledge and truth. Your Creator is the accountant that balances the books of life, and He makes adjustments. So regulated is the divine scheme that spiritually you receive what you have earned, no more and no less. The decision's outcome depends on the stage you have reached by your own efforts. In the things of spirit, there is always perfect adjustment, with no cheating or pretence. The natural law works perfectly, guided by infinite love and wisdom. Each receives what he or she has earned. No one can intervene between cause and effect. Through spreading your divine light and sharing it with others, an obvious blessing has occurred. Live in harmony with the natural law and share your light with humanity, and you will reap the results.

State Twenty: One: Lightworker - Renewal

If you can help one soul to find itself, you have justified your existence. Only one! That is enough!
S. Birch

You have gone through a major awakening and have changed your views from a purely personal point of view to an awareness of all the cosmic influences around you. You have awakened your spiritual eyes and your intuition, which has resulted into the quickening of the spirit. Intuition is the means by which the spirit becomes aware of itself. By trusting your intuition, you have now inner peace and can appreciate the superior side of life. You have learned that it is in the cultivation of the spirit itself that you can attune yourself to higher powers. You can accomplish this through the quietness of your being. Through meditation, you can learn how to attune yourself to all the powers that are round and abound you. At this state, you learn to harmonize your mind with the great minds of the larger life; you learn how to become a better receptor to receive wisdom, inspiration, knowledge and truth. You learn how to tap into all the learning that awaits you and to receive knowledge from the infinite storehouse, which is your Creator. By trusting your Creator, you put yourself in the hands of your Creator and you open your soul to receive the inspiration, which comes from the Creator's reservoir. Now you are the sage and the same power that inspired the prophets of old are inside you. By sharing your knowledge and spiritual truths, your work can light and illuminate with brightness the hearts of those who are tired, disillusioned and depressed.

As it says in the Sefer Yetzira: *All beginnings are rooted in their end and all endings rooted in their beginning.* You are now at the next state in your journey. Having reached enlightenment, your task is to turn back and rouse your fellows. On the threshold of Nirvana, you refuse to enter until all of humanity can enter as well. You have now a new existence and new perspective on life. Your new beginning and new vision is to uplift souls. You are now a Lightworker and your goal is to give comfort and light to individuals who are struggling in darkness. You are now inspired to be an example and to live so that men can recognize that your Creator is working through you. You will react with gratitude through your connectedness with the highest power, which is part of the higher picture and the divine plan. You will be able to react with a gleeful smile and you will spread your wings open and catch the energies coming in towards you with acceptance and gratification. Through a new lease of life, you will raise your hands with pure essences of joy and love and you will embrace yourself so that you know you can achieve whatever you desire. At this state, you desire to be a Lightworker, and to share love, affection, compassion, friendship and sympathy with humanity.

When you give service, you grow your soul and when you touch a soul, you have gained a spiritual victory. Through being a Lightworker, you are enabling the seed of divinity to begin to express itself.

State Twenty Two: Unity - Accomplishment

The locusts have no king, yet go they forth all of them by bands.
Proverbs 30.27

We have come full circle and we have lost all prejudices and fixed ideas. You, the hopeful are now free from the prison of ignorance. The number of completion is twenty-one thus, three times seven, and the number of absolute unitye, infinity, unlimited potential, is the zero which is the number of *the self* and ongoing. Like *the self,* we see things as they are through the eyes and simplicity of a child. You are now serene and devoted to your spiritual growth. Through your spiritual achievements, your actions are now skillful. Your third eye has opened and you have now the certainty that you and your Creator are one and that the divine spark is within you. You have united with your Creator and you have found spiritual truths. Through this unity, your soul has come into its own. By uniting with your Creator, you experience the ecstasy that life can offer for now you live on more than one plane of being. One of life's greatest illusions is that we are a separate unit from God. In this state, you have acquired wisdom that your Creator is not distant and unapproachable, remote, far off, or unreachable, He is in fact a unit within you. You are now aware that you have an infinite spiritual storehouse, endless strength, unlimited power, a reserve, a reservoir and a potency on which you can call whenever you wish. You are profound; your spiritual reality is that you and Shekinah the Infinite Spiritual Presence are an inseparable unit. You have opened yourself up and you have become the recipient of the gifts of spirit within. When you acknowledge God's infinite spiritual presence within you, you can understand and celebrate the meaning of life. You have reached a level of consciousness where you place your trust in your Creator. You know that there is no end and no beginning. There is also no birth and no death; everything becomes accomplished eternally. Compare your life to the miracle of the seasons. The seasons are the eternal circle forever revolving with unbroken constancy. During winter all life sleeps, springtime life awakens; in the fullness of summer, life reveals all its beauty, and during autumn, the voice of nature is hushed and prepares for the sleep of winter when refreshment follows. You need not be a learned person to hear the voice of your Creator. Heavenly voices come more readily to gentle souls in ordinary, plain and down-to-earth people. Our Creator loves unpretentious, honest people. The learned focus on fear and harsh rulings and judgments, while the rest of us hear the soft words of the Creator. When your mind and soul unite with God that is (your divine seed within), it will result into inner peace, inspiration and faith through alignment with your divine will. You are fulfilling yourself when you allow the spirit to manifest in your life. The knowledge that you have gained during this lifetime and the wisdom that you have learned, will be of great value to the life of your immortal soul when you move on to the next stage, eternity.

Chapter 9

The Energy Centers or Chakras in Your Body

In addition to effecting physical wellbeing, chakras may influence an individual's ethical or moral values, and thereby social and collective life as well.

M. Levin

You are now aware that you have to live your life from the inside out and you are conscious of your real self. Now that you have found yourself, you should be wise enough to proceed to develop the divinity, which lies within you. When your spirit is right, then your body will be right, but when your spirit is not right, not in *true alignment*, then your body cannot possibly be right. You should strive to develop your spiritual nature. You are a triune being, meaning trinity as spirit, mind and body. The seed of your foundation is your spirit, which is preeminent. You express your spirit through your mind, which is the *center* of consciousness. Your mind regulates your body, which is your physical machine. Your mind, spirit and body are interrelating factors that affect one another. You cannot have the one without the other, your mind affects your body and your body meets the requirements of your mind.

When your mental and spiritual expressions are limited, it affects your body. You can regulate your body and train your mind to rule the body with a consciousness, an intentional, deliberate consciousness to a height which is yet unknown to the mind and spirit. To gain more knowledge on this you can study the fakirs who have trained themselves to have a complete mastery and discipline over their bodies. This technique is still new to the

Western World although the Muslim mendicant or ascetics have practiced it for ages. Other religions refer to the fakirs as wonder-workers. They perform bodily achievements that we think are impossible. You have to consciously program your physical mind that your mind is the servant of the spirit. You have to get your spirit mind to work, and the rest will follow. This process is not easy. By understanding this and through your awareness, you are now able to take action. Sometimes it takes years of great effort before you will be able to reach the peak. The reason why I am sharing this with you is to make you aware of this process; now that the seed is planted you can investigate further if you wish.

Loads of educational information is available on the energy centers or seven chakras within the body. For our purpose, we need to be aware of these centers, which are the authentic ancient ones, which were laid down by the masters of wisdom. The body has seven major spinning energy centers and many smaller ones that look like spinning wheels or disks, which we call chakras. Each chakra relates to a particular area of the body and they have an affect on the overall functioning of the body. The chakras interact with our emotional, mental, and spiritual energy bodies, thus they help to distribute energy for our physical, emotional, mental, and spiritual functions. Our chakras mediate all energy within, coming into, and going out of our bodies. The seven main chakras are points of greater electromagnetic activity within the auric field. (View the table below). The palms of the hands, the fingers, and the feet are other points of great activity.

Chakras mediate the electromagnetic impulses and other subtle energy impulses of the human energy system. They are not part of the physical body itself but they assist to link the body's subtle energy fields. The state of the subtle energy bodies effects how much or what particular kind of energy finds its way into the body. Each chakra regulates specific frequencies. It influences the area of the physical body around it. It also balances the whole.

Old energy patterns, unresolved issues and circumstances can block your energy centers. When one or more of your chakras are blocked, you are out of balance. Chakras relate to one's relationship and history with those issues. The flow of energy through the chakras is particularly important as it transmits information and holds the memory of thought patterns and feelings. You have to enhance your physical wellbeing and pursue physical, emotional, mental and spiritual growth. For chakras to function properly, you have to clear the paths for the energy to flow freely. Unresolved thought patterns and emotions result in a feeling of exhaustion and hopelessness. You can also experience feelings of divine abandonment and unanswered prayers. When one or more chakra is out of balance or blocked you struggle to find a solution to your problem. To maintain a balanced lifestyle you have to align and balance yourself with your purest of thoughts to be able to operate on a different vibrational level. You have to relax and focus on the center of your being which will tell and guide you how to attune yourself to higher vibrations. You will be able to attract the healing rays and will be successful according to the certain stage of evolution of your soul. Always keep in mind that your body represents the stage that your spirit has attained. All conform to the perfect patterns of the natural law. There are laws within laws; these laws of the universe are infinite. We have to remember that the whole process, the interaction between matter and spirit is complex. You have to experiment with what works for you. The secret is to become still, to listen, and to place yourself on the road of understanding. The power of the spirit is magnetic and you cannot break the magnetic link once you have made contact.

Be kind with yourself when you do not get immediate results. Your body is a complicated machine and your spirit has many facets. All of these are subject to laws that work within laws. Even as harmony rules throughout, within the framework of all these laws there is plenty of interplay and one reacts upon the other.

Here is an example of where or how the changes take place

between a spirit healing force (when you are attuned to healing rays), and the physical change of the body. At some time, there is a linking-up, and the spirit converts into matter. Silver Birch, a Red Indian Spiritual Guide who lived almost three thousand years ago, explained the process as follows: First it depends on the kind of healing that is to be performed. Then he explained that some of us will find it hard to believe, but in some cases, the centers are the old ones laid down by the masters of wisdom. *The 'third eye' and the solar plexus are used because these are centers where body, mind and spirit link up. As an alternative, the subconscious mind of the individual, where it is receptive, is acted upon in such a way so that it is stimulated into sending the necessary chemical reaction to the affected part in a manner that would normally do if health were there and not disease.* S Birch, p18, *The Spirit Speaks*, Psychic Press Ltd, 1995. *The healing force actually flows into the individuals either through the pineal gland or the solar plexus. The vital force streams through the whole being and that is when they feel this warm electrical vibration.* Silver Birch stated that there is no set method; it is all a question of experiment.

How does this help you?

You have to acquire balance, truth and knowledge before you can rise above your realities and daily problems. When one or more chakra is out of balance, your life will be out of balance. You have to take charge of your life and make sure to balance your physical body's requirements including diet, nutrition and exercise, your occupation, relationships, enjoyment, meditation and spirituality on a regular basis. Your energy levels will drop when your lifestyle (the way you live) is out of balance. When you dwell on a short fuse it will result into feelings of inadequacy and failure. When you are exhausted and when you are experiencing low energy levels, it will result in a vicious emotional cycle. Your natural body's cycle and body's rhythm will also be out of balance. When you have blocked chakras, the energies cannot flow freely and willingly through the passages and channels. It is your responsibility to look after yourself and to take appropriate action. You have to begin with the core and discover the inner-inner essence of your being. You have to focus, balance and align yourself with your purest of thoughts. Retreat and take time out for yourself, the first step is to learn how to relax and breathe properly. Listen to calm and uplifting music. Add regular meditation and enjoyment to your schedule. Your purest intentions must be to attract divine vibrations from Source. Teach yourself to balance and align your chakras and soon you will be able to greet a new beginning with new energy awakening within. You will be able to notice new colors around you and you will be in alignment with all the lines of connectedness and communication. Embrace and engage the new balanced energies that will take you to another level of consciousness.

Behavioral Relationship between the Seven-Year Cycles and the Chakras

For you to understand where each chakra is located in the body and what their basic functions are, I have inserted the table below. Study each chakra and its position as well as the functions of the organs. This will give you an idea or starting point on which area you have to focus, when one or more of your chakras are out of balance. Look at the table below and compare your state of being to the seven-year cycles on **p 24**, as well as the functions of each chakra. I have discovered that there may be a behavioral relationship between the seven-year cosmic cycles that govern personal life and the functions of chakras. Keep in mind that each individual is unique. The way the chakras fulfill their functions, in other words, how they interact with each individual's history and development is part of what defines one's energy and wellness.

You have to keep in mind that the behavioral relationship between the basic cycles and the chakras assists you with the overall picture on your status of wellbeing. The manifestations in each individual's life are in accordance with his or her stage of personal and spiritual development. We all have a different life journey and will act in our own unique way to conditions and circumstances which cross our paths be it illness, grievance, pain or injury. The idea that each chakra holds information and history in the mental, spiritual and emotional central parts has implications for our physical wellbeing. Keep in mind that chakras have an influence, but that they do not necessarily cause every illness that relates to your physical body.

The three main causes of disease are – physical, mental and spiritual. Sometimes purely physical causes bring about your condition. For example, you need the skill of a medical doctor to treat you when you break an arm. When something that is purely physical causes your illness, it is easier to deal with it through physical means than through spiritual means.

You have to be aware that everything that happens to you while you are on earth affects your physical body as well as your spirit body. At the same time, everything that affects your spirit body reacts on your physical body; therefore, it is important to balance your chakras. There are forces of action and reaction at work all the time. There is a constant interplay of forces, physically, mentally, and spiritually. This will have an effect on your emotions and your overall wellbeing.

There are diseases that have no real physical causes. The spirit of the person starts some diseases. Selfishness, self-indulgence, greediness and avarice (materialism), for example result in diseases. You have to realize that there are both physical and spiritual causes for disorders. You do not experience real illness in your spiritual body. It is the defect in its adjustment with your physical body. It will affect its vibrations and its relationship with your physical body. Anger for example can affect your spleen area and jealousy the liver, thus the disease in the body will begin to manifest. These behaviors cause maladjustment, which results in distortion of the body's perfect balance as well as a disturbance of the body's harmony. When you are not correctly adjusted and unable to cope with the demands of a social environment, then you are maladjusted. When the body is out of balance and disease causes maladjustment, you will feel unstable, confused, neurotic, disturbed, estranged and alienated. Most of our sicknesses and diseases are self-imposed through negligence and ignorance of the natural laws. Your body is a fine machine and you need to maintain it consistently.

Chakra Table – Name, Position, Function and Organs – Behavioral Relationship

Number, Name & Colour	Position	Function & Organs	Behavioral Relationship between seven- year cycles and chakras
7th Violet / Silver Crown Chakra	This chakra is associated with the area at the top of the head.	Tied to the function of the entire nervous system & skeleton. Influences the Pineal & all nerve pathways & all electromagnetics of the body.	**42-49 and onwards:** Associated with the supreme energy allowing only the purest, most spiritual input into the body. An open crown chakra is a blessing, which means all other chakras are in alignment. You filter thoughts through your heart before you act. Primary focus is on meditation & soul-growth.
6th Indigo Brow / Third Eye Chakra	Located in the middle of the forehead, above the bridge of the nose.	Influences the endocrine system of the body, particularly the Pituitary. Links with immune system & synapses of the brain. Affiliated with organs of perception- nose, eyes, ears, face & brain.	**35-42:** Development of your Third-eye or second sight & perception abilities. More openhearted, understand, accept & embrace others. Focus on spiritual issues; trust your intuition & second sight & clairvoyance through natural development along with the heart chakra. Enlightening input. Use of your gifts appropriately & for the benefit of all. Have a solid spiritual framework. Act with wisdom.
5th Blue Throat Chakra	Located in the throat.	Tied to functions of the mouth, teeth, throat & neck, Thyroid & parathyroid. Affects the respiratory system & functions of the vocal & bronchial system. Issues with throat chakra may reflect eating disorders.	**28-35:** Communication & self-expression, artistic-creative talents & ethical values important. You have now 'a voice'. This chakra has a connection with the 2nd chakra and its cycle. If you have difficulty in expressing yourself it will result in eating disorders = anorexia or compulsive eating (also connected with sexual issues).

4th Green Heart Chakra	Relates to the chest area, between the breasts.	Thymus. Influences the entire immune system, circulatory system & all organs associated with it. Has ties to all heart & childhood diseases & it affects tissue regeneration. Manifestation issues, if blocked.	**21-28:** Maturity = true & mature understanding & use of power - no enforcement. Has achieved wisdom & love. True understanding that people are interconnected. No power struggle & desire to control the other. Free from fight or flight response. Embrace unity = intuition. Welfare of others at heart. Capable of giving & receiving. Focus is on survival of the human race & the planet
3rd Yellow Solar Plexus Chakra	Situated in the solar plexus: in the naval area.	Adrenals. Influences the digestive system & all its organs, assisting the body in the assimilation of nutrients. Affects stomach & intestines the internal organs -pancreas, spleen, liver, kidneys & gallbladder. Working with this chakra can help to ease crippling diseases, intestinal problems & psychosomatic problems.	**14-21:** Gut knowledge. Onset of adulthood, knowledge represents power & authority. Strive to be part of strategic group. Needs to feel secure in his/her knowledge. Individual feel either self-important or feel inferior. Digestion issues = intellectual & emotional issues. Ability to stand your ground when balanced.
2nd Orange Spleen / Naval Chakra	Located halfway between the genitals and the naval. Below the belly.	Adrenals / Spleen & Liver. Tied to the function of the adrenals, influences the reproductive & the entire muscular system of the body. Influences the eliminative system & its organs. Work with this center to assist in detoxifying the body.	**7-14:** Individual associates with larger social unit – think of early teenage years- puberty strikes. Physical, emotional & social issues. If difficulties arise in, or after puberty or problems related to sexual development (including sexual abuse) the adult will suffer. If energy is blocked = diseases reproductive & sexual organs, eating disorders & substance addictions. Lower back = finance problems.
1st Red Base / Root Chakra	Located on the perineum, between the anus and genitals. At the base of spine.	Gonads & Ovaries. Located in the area of the coccyx at the base of the spine. Tied to the circulatory system, reproductive system & the elimination process. Has strong connections with the feet, legs, buttocks & hips.	**1-7:** Infancy & issues of dependence of growth throughout childhood. Focus on basic family unit & wellbeing. Progress towards independence. Emphasis on own needs & desires. Have to find place & harmony with others outside family.

Chapter 10

Personal Wellness

Without divine assistance I cannot succeed: with it I cannot fail.
Abraham Lincoln 1861

Think of your chakras and your neurotransmitters or hormones, as a formidable team, which works consistently to regulate your body's overall functioning and wellbeing.

Personal Wellness is making sure that you are physically, mentally, emotionally and spiritually at your peak. The key to a successful wellness lifestyle is an understanding of the realms of wellness and the factors, which determine wellness. When we understand the realms of wellness, we can apply the way to measure wellness, and, through understanding the factors that determine wellness, we are able to influence it.

Effective individuals journey between realms and levels of wellness all the time. When, in their personal view, they have attained a desired level of mental wellness, they are tending to sense shortcomings in their physical, relational or spiritual wellness. They then, deliberately, through their own free will and choice engage mentally and physically in practices that will shift them to another level or realm of wellness. You have to aspire to experience complete wellness in all four realms and be able to put into practice effective ways to balance your wellness, you can for example: jog, exercise, walk, read, monitor what you eat, do gardening, play games, meditate, pray, visualize, affirm affirmations, take spiritual retreats and sabbaticals, relax and rest or simply have fun. As individuals evolve and sense the beneficial impact of the realms of wellness, so they realize the supremacy of spiritual wellness.

The secret of life is balance, and the absence of balance is life's destruction. Inayat Khan

Effective individuals move between four realms of wellness and balance the flow of activities and energies:

- *Physical wellness* - feeling good and strong from taking care of our bodies with natural nutrition, exercise, preventative measures, natural remedies, restful sleep and relaxation.
- *Mental wellness* - clarity of mind, sharpness of memory, strong self-worth and confidence in one's decision making capabilities and in choosing the right way forward.
- *Relationship wellness* - experiencing loving companionships and having lasting, fulfilling relationships, free from ego and complications.
- *Spiritual wellness* - this derives from harmony between mind, body and soul. It is an ability and consciousness that frees one to experience inspiring emotions and feelings stirred by compassion, love and things of beauty. It is a deep connection with the creations and intelligent design of nature and the universe, acknowledging the presence and power of God in our lives and preparing for the ultimate journey of the spirit. It is honoring the inescapable natural laws and living a life of virtue and integrity.

The Biochemistry of Personal Wellness

My imperfections and failures are as much a blessing from God as my successes and my talents and I lay them both at his feet.
Mahatma Gandhi 1869-1948

Each of us possesses our own unique knowledge of the world and what wellness means to us. We can compare acquiring life's knowledge to the ever-changing seas. We have to understand the world around us by internalizing it through the knowledge and understanding we have acquired from the depths of the ocean of experience. When you transform the fluid of life into understanding, you have removed the physical and you now see the spiritual frame, the foundation of meaning that underlies it.

Neurotransmitters and Receptors
Neurotransmitters and receptors are chemical messengers that profoundly affect our wakefulness, perceptiveness, moods, feelings, memory, thinking and metabolism.
Danie Joubert.

The ever-growing body of neural science and neural psychology has made it possible to better understand wellness. One must realize that the electrochemical processes of the brain are critical to sustained wellness, inspiration and achievement.

Many scientists, philosophers and biographers have researched the chemistry of human behaviors and especially those for sustained health, achievement and success. Their motive in these pursuits has been to make the world a better, nicer and easier place to live in. If we learn from this, we can help eradicate conflict, poverty and hardship.

The world of the mind and the factors that induce success and failure, illness and health have been explored extensively. Neuroscientists concentrate on the effects of childhood traumas and of drugs on individual's neurochemistry. Psychiatrists and psychologists assess the individual's good and bad experiences from birth in order to solve emotional and behavioral problems through psychoanalysis and psychotherapy.

Others concentrated on the effects nutrition has on neurochemistry. Still others concentrate on the effects, which meditation and spirituality have on the neural activity and pathways. The effects which learning, physical exercise, sports and competition have on the mind, have been mapped out. Even occurrences like mass action and crowd behavior are explained in terms of neural stimulation.

One can state with reasonable certainty that personal wellness results from appropriate exercise, nutrition, stimulation, talent use, sacrifice, experience, measurement, recognition and reward. Conversely, deprivation, fear, abuse, malnutrition, ignorance and lack of stimulation (through learning, achievement and challenges) inhibit or slow down personal wellness and destroy health and feelings of achievement, joy, happiness and success.

Our brain cells communicate with one another through an electromagnetic, biochemical message process. Every time we sense something, think, learn or communicate, the neurons (brain cells) in our brains send nerve impulses to billions of other brain cells. You can slow down your thoughts, or give it wings; clear focused thoughts will result in manifesting wellness.

Nerve impulses (electromagnetic, biochemical messages) are fired from one neuron (brain cell) into the receptors of the receiving brain cells via chemical messengers called neurotransmitters. These are made by nerve cells from amino acids, alkaloids and vitamin and mineral co-factors drawn from various places in the body.

When a neuron activates another in this way, it acts like a switch. Neurons fire in sequence and new neural paths are formed by the domino effect. Neuron activity creates the intricate memory traces or neural pathways of the mind. Peak experiences influence the release of neurotransmitters (hormones), resulting in feelings of pleasure, ecstasy and wellbeing.

Neurotransmitters and receptors profoundly affect our wakefulness, perceptiveness, moods, natural cycles, memory, energy levels, thinking and metabolism. Dopamine, serotonin, norepinephrine, epinephrine (adrenalin), and gamma-aminobutyric acid (GABA) are some of the better-known neurotransmitters that affect our feelings, energy, behavior and performance. Neurotransmitters ferry messages from one neuron to another with the brain (*Nash, Time Magazine, 26 May 1997*). The impact of the better-known neurotransmitters on the mind and body are reflected below *(Giannini, 2000:7)*:

- Dopamine: associated with pleasure and elation, it is responsible for cognitive integration, motor activity initiation and working memory.
- Serotonin: associated with feelings of sadness and wellbeing, it is responsible for sleep initiation, mood modulation, pain modulation, theand the modulation of aggression, for controlling anxiety and for maintaining alertness.
- Norepinephrine: responsible for sleep maintenance, mood modulation.
- Epinephrine (adrenalin): responsible for influencing the rate of metabolism, respiratory stimulation and an increase in psychomotor activity. The excitatory effects and exerted upon smooth muscles cells of the vessels that supply blood to the skin and mucous membranes.
- Gamma-aminobutyric acid (GABA): responsible for inhibitory transmission of the cortex; and functions of the cerebellum, hippocampus and limbic system.

Knowing is experience and learning. The more we experience knowing, the more we know. Your internal knowing should now be more spiritual and with substance. The value of the uniqueness of knowing and understanding the realms of wellness and personal wellness will result in the ability for you to take control of your life and your lifestyle. You can now make wise choices on your behavioral patterns and no individual-, group- or any kind of pressure will affect you. It is particularly important to realize that all sensory stimuli, behaviors and experiences have some neural impact and induce neural activity, which influences our wellness and our ability to achieve.

Inspirational Impulses - Peak Experiences

You can have peak experiences through natural stimuli that will have a positive and blissful effect on your state of mind. Choose natural stimuli to influence your neurochemistry such as:

- Breakout achievements: feelings of excitement and ecstasy are inspired by the accomplishment of demanding or challenging, and sometimes-dangerous tasks, such as severe rock climbing, intense abseiling, bungee-jumping, or seeking victory in a major competition. The prospect of a breakout achievement is highly inspirational. Aspirations cause neural activity that leads to cognitive dissonance or tension in the neural pathways. Neural activity continues until equilibrium (balance) is gained. Tension relief follows upon equilibrium. Aspirations are those desires for ownership and achievement which one holds dear.
- Victory: peak experiences from victories (however small) inspire one and create new expectations and desires that induce the further pursuit of achievement.
- Participation: togetherness brings happiness, and celebrations in groups inspire people. Seeing, hearing and participating in joyful occasions and events such as birthdays, Christmases and New Year's parties activate and load new neural pathways with love, excitement, compassion, joy and expectation. Other examples are rallies, non-violent activism gatherings for the greater good, sporting events, celebration parties and religious group participations such as meditation, prayer and worshipping – all these inspire feelings of happiness and contentment.
- Learning and reading: learning new knowledge and skills activates and loads new neural pathways, thus enabling one to be more knowledgeable or skillful. The neural activity induced by learning can cause feelings of great joy and alleviates stress and anxiety.

- Selection: becoming part of a team or the top structure of an organization through selection carries with it a transfer of trust, responsibility and accountability. The neural impact of this transfer is immense, causing excitement, doubt and fear at the same time.
- Good news: sensing (seeing, hearing, feeling, smelling, intuition) images of human wellness and happy tidings induce inspiration. News and visuals of destruction and suffering activate and load new neural pathways with feelings of fear, hate and anxiety and they destroy positive inspiration.
- Praise: when we receive praise for something we did well, we feel exhilarated and invigorated. However, when we are criticized, we experience rejection and our inspiration levels are negatively impacted.

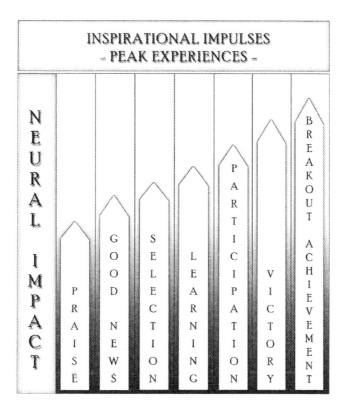

The following factors also influence our neurochemistry, resulting in changes in our inspiration levels:

- Physical exercise: experiencing the pain of exertion modifies the neurotransmitter and receptor activity that induces feelings of relief and achievement. Sensing (seeing, hearing, feeling, smelling) images of people exercising also has implications for mood and feelings.
- Nutrients: everything we eat or drink contains amino acids, alkaloids, minerals and vitamins, which affect the production and secretion (release) of hormones (neurotransmitters) in various places in the body, like the central nervous system, liver and glands. Excesses or shortages of critical nutrients result in modified neural activity.

Drugs: drugs are feeling-enhancing and fantasy-enhancing hormones (neurotransmitters) or receptor replacements or supplements that induce dependency. Abused drugs such as anticholinergics, cannabinoids, dissociatives, opiates, psyche-delics (hallucinogens), sedative-hypnotics, stimulants and volatiles (inhalants) act as antagonists or agonists of hormones and receptors and cause mood and behavior changes.

A strong positive mental attitude will create more miracles than any wonder drug. Patricia Neal

We experience positive reinforcement and inspiration from sensory inputs that give us joy and that excites the glands or energy centers in the body and mind. The diagram below illustrates the effects of sensory inputs. Good news, for example, activates the release of the neurotransmitter (hormone) Dopamine, which is associated with pleasure and elation.

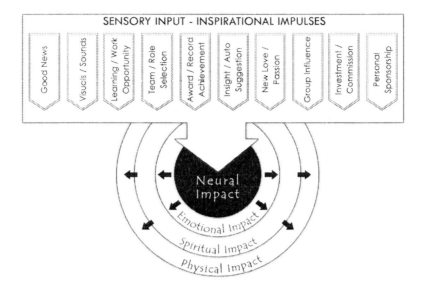

How do you apply the above knowledge to your own wellbeing?

You are now aware that your chakras and hormones work in harmony with one another and why it is cardinal to keep them in balance to acquire a healthy lifestyle to maintain personal wellness. During your life's journey, you have to choose between compromise and freedom.

Always remember that you create within yourself whatever conditions you want. The law is perfect and the law of attraction will attract whatever you focus on. The law does not only work for good, it also works the other way. All laws, which you can use for the greatest service, can also be abused. As high as you can rise just as low you can sink. It all depends on the way you choose to apply yourself to the perfect laws. Thus: As low as you can fall, in the same way can you rise to the greatest heights.

Our will must be impressionable before the will of the Creator. You have to choose a lifestyle of virtuous living. One of the realities of life is constant turmoil. We have to choose how we are going to manage these realities. Through balancing your chakras and your hormones you will be able to sense that you are in charge of you and that you can achieve whatever you desire. You are unique, exceptional, a gift, and a special being from the light.

You are now conscious of your limitations and yet you are aware of your strengths and your powers. You have the wisdom that you will be healthy when you live a righteous life, when your thinking is right, and when your spirit, mind and body are harmonious. You know that you are a spiritual being and to achieve personal wellness you have to live a balanced life. You can empower yourself! Hold on to the above essentials. Do not allow yourself to be out of focus or diverted. When you experience problems and confusions or when you stress and you are out of balance, retire, and relax within where the peace and power of God dwell. In the silence and hush of the spirit, within, you will find all the answers that you seek. Use all your resources and take all the time that you need to heal yourself. You are magnificent. You are spirit in miniature. You already have all the keys and tools that you need. Create a safe comfortable place for yourself, where you can meditate and focus go within for at least 45 minutes. When we find solutions to our problems, we can compare it to finding keys to open doors. A key helps us to make life easier to open doors. Through finding our inner key to open doors, it will help us to heal ourselves. Sometimes we struggle to find keys. Keep in mind that all searches begin within you, thus inside oneself. In the previous chapters, we have discussed that we can compare our physical life in this lifetime to the school of life. You are a student among other students. Be aware that in this chapter you are going to graduate and receive the *Key of Health and Personal Wellness*. When you enroll and accept this challenge, you have to be willing to learn, grow, and take action wherever you need to maintain, or repair your mind, body or spirit for personal wellness.

Meditation-Key of Health and Personal Wellness
I am going to guide you in doing a short self-analysis meditation

to assist you in finding keys to balancing and healing yourself. This is an easy practical meditation. Remember that only you can findhave the answers that are within you. You are the master of your thoughts and destiny. Read the steps and then follow them by repeating them in your own mind. Begin by closing your eyes and taking deep breaths. Take a few seconds to relax and focus on the core of your being. Be aware that your teacher is now in front of you, and is now handing you the manuscript and content page for the outcome you desire. Look with eagerness and interest at the various topics, chapters and keys. Take a moment to absorb the content and discuss it with your teacher if you have any questions. You are entitled to receive special treatment from your teacher, and you are favored right now. For a moment, focus on your goal, that is graduation day which is your primary goal. Visualize how you feel when they call your name and when all your friends are giving you a standing ovation. Pour in all the positive uplifting feelings. Feel a different person and pour the love essence with care and compassion into your heart centre and bath in it with a beautiful smile on your face and focus on the main artery pouring in the love and sending it to the rest out there.

Now you can return to your seat and focus on your degree. Open it slowly – what does it say? Are there any instructions that you have to follow? If so make mental notes – take time to understand and ponder on the notes. What are your achievements? What are your strengths and weaknesses? At what do you excel? You are a perfect child of God; take time to think about this spiritual truth!

As a graduation gift you receive a beautiful Château and new coupé from your loved ones. You have earned it and got the master key to the large country house and the sports car. Only you can drive this vehicle and only you know the way forward. You are going to explore new roads and only you know which way to go, where to turn, and which path to follow to the Château fortress. You decide which way to go and as you follow the curves, you will arrive safely at your new destination. Take your master key and unlock the front door of your mansion while you explore the surroundings and the inside. Do you need to repair or maintain any parts of the house? Do you need to make changes such as to rebuild or fix some of the rooms? You are capable! Go down to the basement of your building to find your master toolbox that is your treasure chest. All the tools for maintaining your health and repairing your body are in your treasure chest. Take your master key and open your box. Inside you will find a list of all the things you should focus on to repair and balance your physical body. The most important thing is to have positive thoughts, and a healthy mindset that will help you to be able to operate on a different vibrational level. A healthy mind will guide and tell you of how to operate in a way that will make you feel a different person. It will help you to do something to repair your body, which will help you to make a difference in your life and to shift a new image for you into place. Your new consciousness will give you the inner knowing that you can trust and believe in the new image you portray in your mind knowing that it is from your Creator.

You have to now change your lifestyle and put in the effort to make changes on the things on your list to achieve personal wellness. You need to do whatever it takes to be happy and satisfied with your final product. Your responsibility is to eliminate anything that you know that you have to destroy and defeat. Compare the process to a parasite or nuisance that threatens and terrorizes your survival. You do not need to use poison to eliminate parasites and undesirable circumstances. Mentally make the decision that it is time to move on from the old and to embrace the new. You have to let go intellectually and mentally and stay detached from the old situation. When your mind, body and spirit are in harmony, you will feel healthy and able to resist mental irritations and temptations. Irritations and temptations will go away for they will dwell where they are welcome. They are not able to survive in a healthy house where the focus is to thrive on love, joy, compassion, beauty, integrity, virtue and service to humanity and Spirit. They thrive on addictions, resentment, anger, stress, depression, unforgiveness, backstabbing, lies, chaos, confusion, disorder and hatred.

Search your house and if you find any of these unwanted feelings, temptations, problems or addictions, consciously act and decide to take immediate action to eliminate them. When you awaken within, you discover truth and you open the right channels to receive the correct vibrations for the inner healing to take place. Visualize how you deposit these unwanted feelings and desires into the trash-can. It is your responsibility to release and to get rid of the symptoms that have been in you for such a long time be able to adjust to normality. Forget about the way it was handed out and set yourself free, as it is the past chapters of your life. Fret not the ups and downs of life for it is part of the cycles of life. In order for you to be able to move forward you have to erase the emotional state that you find yourself in. Remember that you can be your own best friend and that the divine spark is with and in you. Accommodate and embrace the divine energy within you. Focus now on the present and exciting future chapters of your life. Embrace the new beginning and trust and believe that it is for your highest good. You are a survivor in your own right. All the challenges that you have faced have made you stronger and wiser. You can do it, and in return, your reward will be to receive love, acceptance, forgiveness, spiritual truth and peace from yourself. The process is not mechanical but a process of inner healing and self-acceptance. You are in the process of restoring your self-worth and the love needs to come from within you and not from someone else. Make sure that that which you weave into the foundation of your being is according to the divine pattern. Gaze into the mirror at your reflection and affirm: *I love you!* Give yourself a hug and a smile with acceptance. Affirm the following out loud. *I promise to treat you with the utmost respect and care that you deserve. You are a wonderful and perfect child of the Light. You are a spiritual being and reflect the greatness of your Creator.* Let us remember why God created us. Let us strive to do nothing, which will bring a blemish or stain to thatour divine association, so that always we qualify for the blessing and approval that comes to all who are linked in unity of purpose with The Creator of all life. Know that you have Heaven's support and stay focused on the road to recovery.

Part II

Every visible thing in this world is put in charge of an angel.
Saint Augustine great philosopher and theologian 354- 430

Chapter 11

The Inescapable Natural Laws

The Great Spirit is the Law. Know that, and you have learned life's greatest secret, for once you realize the world is governed by unchangeable, unbreakable, immutable, omnipotent law, you know that justice is done and none can be forgotten in the great scheme of creation.

S. Birch – 1938

We all need a clear understanding of the universe in which we live. Law rules the whole universe and all of its existence. When we discussed *The Spirit*, we have touched on the supreme power which directs the whole universe and us and beyond, through the natural laws. The universe is ruled and expressed through God's unchanging perfect laws, which God has ordered to operate in precision. These laws control every facet of all the activities throughout the whole universe. Nowhere in the whole universe is there absence of the supreme natural laws. God has forced His divine will through His divine ordinance. You have to awaken to the reality that God is in charge; He regulates the law, which is compulsory. There is no other way, you have to adjust and honor God's natural perfect laws if you want to advance your soul- growth. Be assured that there is no happening left to chance or mistake. The divine law regulates and controls everything and the divine law considers every happening. The law is perfect and no one can intervene in the unalterable sequence of cause and effect.

In this chapter, we are going to discuss our relationship between this supreme power, which is in fact the law, and we are going to discuss our relationship between the natural law and one another. In advance, God has equipped us with all the knowledge that we need to attune ourselves to higher vibrations for assistance, which is a part of the natural law. It is your responsibility to learn to respond to vibrations of the highest planes of spirit through honoring the laws. As you awaken to this awareness and spiritual truth, you will find the precious gemstones and diamonds of your spirit within yourself. You will know that God has provided in advance all the forces of goodness, helpfulness and service at your side to guide, help and inspire you. As you unfold your spirit, you will draw yourself closer to God, thus you will live a virtuous life in unison with His laws.

It is essential that you now know and believe that you are a spiritual being and that you are not only human, but also divine. It will be much easier for you to live your life in harmony and to trust your inner knowing which will result in devoted faith. You have to consciously affirm daily that you are a spiritual being and you have to trust in the divine power within. As humans, we have little faith in the power within for the mere fact that we do not walk our talk! The law is perfect and we cannot alter the law. You have to stop to look for peace and solutions without, and you have to learn to find the eternal peace and solutions within. You can only find true peace when you live in harmony with the natural laws of cause and effect, and when you honor these laws.

In Silver Birch Anthology, he teaches us that all law is part of one vast law. To him God is the law and the law is God. The law is perfect in its operation. The Webster's international dictionary describes perfect as supreme excellence, zero defect, fault or flaw. Think about it and ponder on the magnificence of perfection. Think of brilliance, majesty, radiance, glory and splendor. When I think of my Creator, I think about all the above. I see in my minds' eye perfection and magnificence! Now you can see and understand why the natural law is perfect and why *God Himself* is the perfect supreme law in operation.

Everything works in harmony, for all are part of the divine

plan. The law teaches us to look for our salvation through learning the lessons of cause and effect. We have to work it out in our daily lives. Each and every one throughout the world has to throw away all the false religious studies that teach them that it is possible to direct on to others the results and responsibilities of their actions. You alone are the cultivator and horticulturist of your soul. God has provided you with all the keys, tools and everything that you need to grow in wisdom, grace and beauty. Study figure 7, the divine survival kit again. You have the expertise and all the equipment, gear and implements; you have to use them well and wisely and apply your skill to acquire results and grow your soul. God has provided you with the spiritual tree of life.

Effect always follows cause with exact and accurate precision. It means that effect follows with mathematical accuracy and correctness. Again, we have perfection and zero defects. No individual - (no matter what class, designation, grade, position, rank, color, label or title) has the power to alter by one hairbreadth (a tiny part) the sequence of cause and effect. The greatness of the law is that we have to account for ourselves. When you break the law, you will pay the price, on the other hand, when you live within the law you will reap the benefits and the rewards! There are many sets of laws operating, some controlling the physical, some the mental and others the spiritual, sometimes and occasionally all of these are interlocking. A sad truth is that most of us do not appreciate the truths of spirit and the result of cause and effect in our lives; we wait until the last stage of our lives to awaken to the realities of the spirit and the realities of the natural law. Take into account that you cannot force soul- growth and the sooner you awaken to the realities of life the better for you to learn and grow. When you wait too long, you may feel that it is too late for your soul to find itself, and you efforts are hopeless Make a contract with yourself today that you are going to be in charge of your life. What you focus on grows.

Be committed to honor the natural laws thus: Write the date and put your signature next to it in ink, then put it up at a special place where you can see it daily. Read and verbalize your affirmation. Through daily visualization, you will stimulate your affirmation (to honor the natural laws) and you will restore your determination to accomplish your goal through your positive thoughts and affirmations.

Be committed to your goal and reap the reward of having a clear plan with good intentions, which will result in a clear vision. A clear vision will give you confidence, which in return, will boost your morale.

Various Important and Fundamental Natural Laws

Law #1: The Divine Law of Compensation

You have to experience adversity in various forms to grow your soul. View these adversities as blessings. This statement may sound like a cliché but one of the fundamental spiritual truths is that the greater the suffering that you have to go through, the greater is the knowledge and soul- growth that you receive in return. The knowledge that we receive when we are hurt, or when we experience pain and sorrow results into an internal knowing which is more spiritual than substance. This is where the law of compensation has an effect on us. Our Creator is our accountant, the books of life are always balanced, and He makes adjustments according to the stage we have reached through our own efforts and through applying the natural laws in our lives. The divine system is perfectly regulated, that in return spiritually you receive just what you deserve, no more and no less. You can only receive what you have earned and you cannot cheat or pretend. Your Creator is the accountant and He always acts with infinite love and infinite wisdom. There is never any abrogation, suspension or interference of the law. The Creator is the law, which is perfect, supreme and constant! This perfect law does not work on accidents, likelihood or chance. The compensation of the law is the reward for virtuous living and true and honorable actions. You get the reward for what you have done in harmony with the natural law and not for what you say or believe that you have done.

Law #2: The Eternal Natural Law – Law of Cause and Effect

The natural law is constant and steady, it never varies or fluctuates and you cannot change the natural law. You cannot opt out of the natural law, which means that the law is compulsory to all. The Creator is the law and the threshold, the essence and the personification of the law; you cannot shift, modify, move, negotiate or plead with the law. When you live in harmony and in tune with the law, you will harvest the rewards. You will also pay the price when you live against the law. The law operates on cause and effect meaning you will reap what you sow. Think of any seed and know that all seeds are true to its type. When you sow potato seeds, you will harvest potatoes. You cannot expect to harvest tomatoes. You can pray 24/7 hours to harvest tomatoes, the result will be the same, you will harvest potatoes, and you cannot have it any other way. This principle applies with exact precision on your daily actions. You can only cultivate that which you have sown. The natural law of cause and effect is inevitable, inexorable, unavoidable and unalterable.

Law #3: The Natural Law of Eternal Supply – Law of Attraction

What you focus on grows. Most individuals have fear in their hearts and they focus on negativity. When you are afraid of not getting results, the element of fear disturbs your vibrations. You block your heart centre, which results in difficulty to manifest. You have to open your heart and focus on perfect love, which will attract the right vibrations. When you focus on perfect love, it will demolish your fearful feelings. *Seek first His kingdom and His right-eousness, and all these things shall be yours as well.* Matthew 6.33. When you put the law of attraction into operation, you will attract the results abundantly. The results have to come when you allow the law to function. Jesus has taught us that we are blessed when we believe and we have not yet seen, but thrice blessed are they who know, and because they know, they have placed their faith in that which they cannot yet see. Through this dedicated faith, the Creator will always provide for your basic needs. You will have clothes, food and shelter. When you live right and have devoted faith you will be able to participate in the reward of your Creator. It is your responsibility to trust and to believe that you live and move under the protection of your Creator and His laws.

Law #4: The Natural Law of Transcendence - Law of Action and Reaction

This law operates hand in hand with the above law of attraction. Think of it as an extension of the law although it functions on its own. Always keep in mind that there are many laws operating within laws. When you worry and when you focus on fear your physical body loses its vitality. Because you are a spiritual being expressing yourself through your physical body, you are closing the sliding gates to your body. They control the volume of flow to your body and you cut yourself off from the source of supply when you stress and when you are fearful. Your body acts according to the natural law of action and reaction. When you are nervous, anxious, terrified, frightened or scared, you inhibit the correct vibrations to come through. You have to learn to control your fears and to rise above your reality to attain self-mastery. Worry inhibits your spiritual atmosphere/aura and disturbs the psychic vibrations. The correct power from source cannot flow through until you remove the blockage. You have to train your mind to focus on the correct vibrations to be able to receive. You have to refuse to let your fear dominate you. Turn your face upwards and affirm: I am a fragment of God and I am indestructible! God favors me! My Creator adores me! It is easy and natural to receive.

Sometimes your circumstances and physical surroundings are so severe that it feels as if your have a crushed spirit, this results in an illusion that you cannot rise above your situation. Feelings such as anxiety, nervousness, stress, tension and trauma imprison your manifestation ability. Focus on your faith, trust in your Creator, and have the certainty that you can overcome all your problems. To be able to conquer your reality you have to train your mind to be clear and focused, thus you will be able to attract the correct vibrations from Source. To attain self-mastery you have to discipline yourself to consciously go through rigorous training and persist so that you are able to rise above and surmount your circumstances. You are the master of your thoughts, words and actions.

Law #5: The Natural Law of Physical Wellbeing – Law of Intention and Motive

Earlier we discussed physical wellness and the effect of sensory stimuli, our behavior and how to maintain a healthy body. You are aware that your physical body is remarkable and complex and that you have to give it the right attention through rest, diet, nutrition, mental wellness and exercise. When you live in harmony with the natural laws, you will not have ailment, disease and illness. Disease results when you experience disharmony. Your intentions are of overriding consideration and when you break the law, you will harvest the results and the law will produce the penalty. You cannot punish your body and have the illusion that you will not pay the price. When you see or experience danger signs that your body is weak you have to pause and reflect on how to re-charge and revitalize. You have to cherish your physical body and monitor your energy levels on an on-going basis. When you neglect your body, it will stop. With efficient rest and recuperation, your body will be able to resume its efficiency. Your body acts on the natural law of cause and effect. It is your responsibility to provide and nurture your body with the essentials to perform its daily tasks. This brings our attention to suicide. You should not quit the physical plane before your spirit is ready for the next stage. The law has made provision and you will cut yourself off from your loved ones. Only your Creator knows when you are ready to move on to the next stage. When you damage your physical body, you will reap the results. All action results into a domino effect.

Law #6: The Natural Law of Incentive – Soul- Growth - Riches Within, versus Materialism and Wealth

Every emotion, lesson and experience that you have acquired and accumulated during your life on earth contributes to your soul-growth. This law works hand in hand with the divine law of compensation. Think of both sides of the coin. The Creator rules over material and spiritual possessions, there are no divisions in His universal realm. If you want to grow your soul, you have to realize that, that which is material and spiritual are not separate and different. The things of matter react on the things of spirit and visa versa. Both are parts of one inseparable life. You always pay a price. When you focus on growing your spirit, the reward will be evolution of your soul. In addition, the gift for applying intuition is increased sensitiveness and insight. On the other hand, when you focus on accumulating material wealth, you will be rich in possessions but poor in spiritual riches. Your focus needs to be on growing your spirit and not to collect only material wealth. You cannot accumulate only material wealth and neglect your spirit without paying the price. When you focus on being a Lightworker and you serve humanity, you draw yourself closer in union with your Creator and the incentive is perfect peace within. The riches within, is receiving God's perfect unconditional love and divine approval, which results into perfect peace. The incentive, which you receive, is that God surrounds you with His ultimate love. When you honor the law the reward will be receiving the essentials for your wellbeing and soul- growth. The Creator, which is the infinite supreme power, has provided for the universal laws to operate through love and wisdom.

Law #7: The Natural Law of Awakening

When you awaken to the greatest riches of the spirit, you will not judge the smaller things and happenings on earth because you know that you are preparing yourself to see and experience the greater things when you move on to the next stage of life. The kingdom of heaven is within you and you are on earth to build your character, grow your soul, finding truth and prepare for eternity. How you face adversity, problems, hardship and difficulty is how you build your character. It is a certainty and fundamental spiritual truth, that no problem of the world is greater than the power within you. When you awaken to the fact that you are a fragment of God and you find the kingdom of heaven within, you are untouchable to the problems of the world. Then you live in harmony with the Creators' law. You can only find this power within the soul. You have to awaken to the permanent and lasting effects of the spirit, when you focus on the temporary joys of earth, you confuse yourself and slow-down your soul- growth. You will not escape your punishment, and you will not loose your reward depending on what you focus on. As we have discussed in the previous chapters, the law is perfectly balanced and you cannot cheat the law. You have to awaken and grow your soul to receive the reward. Jesus taught many years ago that we have to be in the world but not of the world. The human part of you belongs to the world but the divine part of you belongs to your Creator. The reward for awakening is evolution of the soul and preparation for eternity.

Law #8: The Natural Law of Justice

Now that we have established that God is the supreme, perfect, omnipotent law, we know that perfect justice is a reality. The truth is that God knows and records everything. No action or deed can be misplaced, vanish or disappear. That is why every facet of life finds its place in the universal realm. God, which is the law, embraces everything. Our Creator overlooks nothing and justice is always done. The Creator as the law, which is in power, is supreme and controls everything. Sometimes our free will creates confusion and obscures the working of the law in our own minds. Remember that the law exists just the same and is perfect in operation. It is consistent, reliable, unfailing and never changes. Perfect justice is compulsory through the natural law of cause and effect. For example: Some of us have the illusion that we can wipe away our sins in a flash. God cannot miraculously wipe away all your sins when you have lived a sinful life for let's say fifty years. No deathbed regrets and remorse will save you. You cannot escape or cheat the perfect, supreme law. You will reap what you have sown!

Law #9: The Natural Law of No Interference

Sometimes through our own ignorance (that we are not aware of), we ask through prayer for things which are not good for us or which our soul has not yet earned. This is where the law of no interference comes into effect. Our Creator cannot provide us with things, which are not good for us, thus our prayers cannot be answered. These are the times when we learn most about life. Assess and look back on your life and recall something that you wanted desperately at the time only to find out later that it was a blessing not receiving what you have asked for. We have to grow and learn continually or we will stagnate. Adversity and sorrow tests one's strength of belief. It takes endurance and fortitude to stand up to adversity. At the time when you experience the feeling of unanswered prayer, you have to stand your ground, and free yourself from the illusion that it is impossible to find a solution to your problem. These kinds of thoughts and feelings are self-imposed, it is your free will, which creates the confusion and makes it difficult to see the solution. It also obscures the working of the law of attraction in your mind. It is your responsibility to explore new ways of thinking. Your soul will only grow when you are willing to step outside your comfort zone. The hardest part of the Creators' task is to sometimes stand by and to see us suffer, He knows that He cannot send us help because only then can we benefit and grow. The spiritual and eternal rewards are much greater when we evolve our souls through having patience and determination to overcome and resolve our adversities. Our Creator is aware that He cannot help for you are experiencing the battle with your own spirit. While you are going through these battles, your Creator is closer to you than you can imagine. He is experiencing and fighting the battle with you and He protects and guides you with infinite love and wisdom. This is the law of no interference. Let the wise words of Mother Theresa comfort you when she reminds you that to keep a lamp burning, you have to keep putting oil in it. When the law of no interference dawns on you, you have to become quiet, reflect and go within. Through the silence of your mind, your heart will direct you on the path that you must follow. You will find reassurance and determination and you will have gained the wisdom that there is always a better future. Your guardian angels, guides and those who love you may not interfere with your free will and they cannot solve your problems for you. If they tell you what to do, they will interfere with the law and your free will and your progress will suffer. You need to make your own choices, the troubles and trials on your path are challenges that you need to face and conquer. The forces of goodness, service and helpfulness will assist you with love and guidance and they will celebrate with you, your victory!

Law #10: The Natural Law of Healing

True healing is a soul process and it is not a physical occurrence, which means that when your soul is ready the healing will take place. You can have no relapse when you have accomplished true healing. The law is unalterable and the law is perfect which is neutral, automatic, inflexible and divinely ordained. When you open and awaken your spirit to receive God's healing vibrations, you are awakening your slumbering, dormant spirit to begin to express itself through your intention. When you awaken you become conscious. When you truly become conscious you have increased your inner wisdom and knowledge. Through awakening, you can accomplish self-change. Thus, you are attracting the healing rays through the natural law of attraction. When you do that, then the natural, self-recuperating processes of the body gets to work and results in health. You have opened the channel to receive the flow of healing light to your spirit from your Creator. You Creator in return overwhelms you with healing light, compassion, mercy and kindness.

Law #11: The Spiritual Law

When you share spiritual truths, you illuminate and help to heal the world and in return, God surrounds you with divine protection. This is the spiritual law in action. The key is to give love and service to your Creator, humanity, the animal kingdom and the environment through unconditional, selfless love and true compassion. The reward of the spiritual law is that God graciously showers you with His abundant blessings and your soul rises to a higher level. You are a Lightworker!

Law #12: Manmade Laws

When we deal with our Creator's laws we have to be crystal clear that they are supreme. You cannot think, compare, judge, associate, evaluate or weigh the manmade laws against God's flawless laws. The perception in today's life is that most laws protect the unlawful and it is associated with red tape, endless effort and crooked justice or no justice at all. Be assured that God is the ultimate accountant and that He always balances the scale. No one can buy his way out, or opt out of these supreme laws. You will reap what you have sown.

Chapter 12

Divine Plan

Evil is the absence of God in people's hearts, it is the absence of love,
humanity and faith. Love and faith are like heat and light. They exist.
Their absence leads to evil.
Albert Einstein 1879-1955

Through our conscious awareness that we are spiritual beings and through receiving knowledge on the natural laws, we can make fruitful and uplifting choices that will contribute to our soul- growth. Through our awareness, we are able to make the world a better place by honoring the laws, and by living a virtuous life, which will give service to all God's creatures, human, animal or whatever form they take and in return reflects service to our Creator. You now have to choose between the things that are right and the things which are wrong. Your actions portray either wisdom when you work with God's laws or ignorance when you choose to work against them. When we are ignorant, it means that we have a lack of perception of knowledge, wisdom or intelligence. Ignorance means that you are unaware and uninformed or unenlightened. You are destitute of knowledge and the quality or state of your being is ignorant. When you choose to act on wisdom, you experience the perfect laws as a blessing instead of an inconvenient truth. The Divine Plan unfolds itself constantly. The wise individual, wise because you have the knowledge, learns to co-operate with your Creators' infinite love and wisdom.

A part of God's divine plan for your life is to assist you to open your spiritual eyes and to have a desire to reach out to receive greater knowledge. This does not happen easily; to be able to attain spiritual wisdom agony will inevitably accompany you, physically, mentally or spiritually. The reward is receiving spiritual truths (the good news and true gospel), which leads to hope, peace, harmony and light that God wants to share with you. Some of us through our upbringing, religion and belief-system have to reprogram our minds to be able to erase misrepresentations. It can be challenging to oppose established dogmas and doctrine. You have to think outside your conventional framework and challenge the add-ons and additions of religion to find the ultimate spiritual truth. For centuries, a superstructure was built upon false statement of beliefs that has resulted in selfishness and ignorance worldwide. The result and effect is a world that is spiritually barren, insolvent and confused.

The great soul Mahatma Gandhi said that *God has no religion* and through his wisdom he proclaimed: *I believe in the fundamental Truth of all the great religions of the world. I believe that they are all God given. I came to the conclusion long ago... that all religions were true and also that all had some error in them.*

God's divine plan is to restore our reason and to replace false impressions with truth, superstition with knowledge and darkness with light. The divine plan is to shower us with spiritual truth, knowledge and wisdom that will result in trusting our own supreme intelligence. Your supreme intelligence is your divine reason, which is the hallmark of your Creator. When you trust your reason, you awaken to a new life, which is the new beginning of entering the freshness of spring. New beginnings liberate you and increase your awareness of the eternal foundation on which all life in the whole cosmos rests. It also gives you the knowingness that you are protected with God's invisible shield, which is around you. Through this awakening and knowingness, you enhance your inner life and your inner radiance. With new assurance, you are able to project an inner glow and inner confidence. You are now able to share truth with love, which will be embraced.

Throughout the ages, we have had saints, great philosophers, visionaries, reformers; the great master, seers and all the idealists who had noble and elevated ideas. All these great souls have, through living their passion and truest interest, endorsed and honored God's divine plan to render a service to humanity and the environment. Even today, we are inspired and motivated by the riches that they left behind. It is our responsibility to follow their example. H. Jackson Brown, Jr. said *Live so that when your children think of fairness, caring and integrity, they think of you.* I want to take it further; you should reflect the above continuously. When someone has met you the reply must be. *What a privilege and honor to have met such a great Lightworker!*

I would like to share with you the profound insight that Albert Einstein shared with us during his early years when he was a young student. Einstein has become synonymous with *Genius.* He was a theoretical physicist, who won the Nobel Prize in physics for the discovery of the law of the photoelectric effect. The 1999 Time Magazine called him the Person of the Century.

During a discussion in class at a university, a professor asked his students if God created everything whereby the answer was a confident yes. Pleased with the answer he then said that through their reply, they had confirmed that God created evil as well. The professor wanted to prove that faith was only a myth.

The young Einstein decided to challenge the professor and asked the professor if he would be willing to answer his question, which the professor agreed upon. He then asked the professor if 'cold' existed whereby the reply was a definite yes from the professor. Einstein corrected the professor by telling him that cold does not exist. He then explained that according to studies in Physics, cold is the total and complete absence of heat. An object can only be studied if it has and transmits energy, and it is the heat of an object that transmits its energy. Without heat, the objects are inert, incapable to react. Therefore, cold does not exist. We created the term cold to explain the lack of heat.

Einstein then asked the professor if darkness existed whereby the professor again replied yes. The young student told the professor that he was again wrong, because darkness is the total absence of light. You can study light and brightness, but not darkness. The prism of Nichols, shows the variety of different colors in which the light can be decomposed according to the longitude of the waves. Einstein then confirmed that darkness is the term that we created to explain the total absence of light. The young Einstein then corrected the professor's earlier statement and he told him that God did not created evil. *Evil is the absence of God in people's hearts; it is the absence of love, humanity and faith. Love and faith are like heat and light. They exist. Their absence leads to evil.* Albert Einstein. The professor was amazed and speechless by this profound statement.

A fundamental part of God's Divine Plan is that every human being on earth has to have all access to all the knowledge and necessities to be able to prepare their mortal bodies for eternity. This means that true knowledge needs to be within reach to all, to be able to prepare for spiritual growth and to be able to live in harmony with the natural laws. It is everyone's divine birthright to have all the supplies of life freely available and accessible. Gods' intention is that we have to get our bodies in perfect shape, meaning we have to accomplish self-mastery through connecting matter and spirit. When you read Jeremiah 29:12-13 it confirms that you have to seek God and in return, He gives you His guarantee that you will find Him. *Then shall ye call upon me, and ye shall go and pray unto me, and I will hearken unto you. And ye shall seek me, and find me, when ye shall search for me with all your heart.* Through connecting, you will have balance, rhythm and harmony and you will accomplish wholeness. One of your primary goals in life must be to strive to live a nobler and virtuous life and to always help to uplift your *species*.

You have the assurance and guarantee that an essential part of the divine plan is that your Creator is watching over you, this is a spiritual fact. Jeremiah 29.11 confirms this statement: *For I know the thoughts that I think toward you, saith the LORD, thoughts of peace, and not of evil, to give you an expected end.*

You are the image of God. I would like to share the following story with you.

You are the image of God. Malachi 3.3. When you read the passage in the Bible it says: *He will sit as a refiner and purifier of silver.* Ponder on the words and think back on when we had discussed the alchemist, who turns base metal into pure gold or silver. This statement shares information with us on the character and nature of our Creator. To get a better understanding of the meaning, we have to find out about the process on refining silver, thus we have to 'meet' a silversmith. Imagine that you have an appointment with a silversmith and that you are watching him. As you watch the silversmith, focus on the piece of silver in his hand, which he holds over the fire while he heats it up. The silversmith explains the following to you, without looking at you, as he holds the piece of sliver with care in his hand over the heat. In refining silver, you need to hold the silver in the center of the fire where the flames are extremely hot to be able to burn away all the impurities. Compare yourself to the silver and see your Creator holding you tightly in His hand when you experience adversity and when it feels like being in such a hot spot. Now ponder on your Creator's guarantee: *He sits as a refiner and purifier of silver.* The guarantee is that God never, not for a second, take His eyes off you. Focus on the silversmith again who has to sit in front of the fire the whole time watching the silver while it is being refined. The silversmith explains that he not only has to sit there while holding the silver, he also has to keep his eyes on the silver the entire time while it is in the fire. The silversmith cannot leave the silver for a moment too long in the hot flames, if he does, he will destroy the silver. Now think of the natural laws, which work with exact precision. God never takes His eyes off you, not even for a second. You are the only person who through the lack of knowledge may think that God has deserted you, while you are going through difficult times. Now we can ask the silversmith our final question: How do we know when the silver is fully refined? Our silversmith smiles with compassion and gives the following answer: *Oh, that's easy - when I see my image in it.*

It is your responsibility to strive to be the best that you can be and to have the knowledge that you are the image of your Creator. If today you are feeling the heat of the fire, remember that God has His eye on you and He will keep watching you until He sees His image in you. He has made provision for you in His divine plan and He gave you His guarantee that you will always be protected and taken care of. At birth, your Creator equips you with a Divine Survival Kit, which is the **Spiritual Tree of Life** that helps you to succeed in life.

1. We are spiritual beings and are created in the image of God. Read Genesis 1.27. The link that binds us together is the link of divinity. You are directly connected to your Creator thus you have all the love, power, potential, inspiration and abilities to be great and perfect.
2. Our Creator has equipped us with our reason to decide and discern what is true and what is not true. Refuse and decline what your reason cannot accept, no matter from who it comes or the source.
3. Thirdly you are blessed with intuition. Your intuition is your inner voice or gut feeling; trust your intuition, it is never wrong. In Emmanuel's book Pat Rodegast says: *I have learned we hear with our hearts, not our ears, we understand with our intuition, not our minds.*
4. Listen to your heart and filter all thoughts through your heart

center before you act.

5. Our Creator gave us a few basic inescapable, supreme, divine, natural laws, which operates on cause and effect. We have a build-in compass to give us guidance on what is right and what is wrong. When you live with the laws you benefit, when you live against the laws you pay the price.

6. At birth you are given helpers to stay with you and assist you during your time on earth. Angels, guides, diseased loved ones and divine helpers are always with you to help and protect you.

Your Creator is not inaccessible, unattainable, unreachable, unapproachable, remote, and hard to find. It is your responsibility to connect with Him through faith (born out of the knowledge that you have accumulated so far), prayer and meditation. Know that you are a tiny part of Him. You are the image of God. Aspire to grow into a Lightworker and to live a life of virtue. Below is an illustration, which I call the spiritual tree of life.

Spiritual Tree of Life

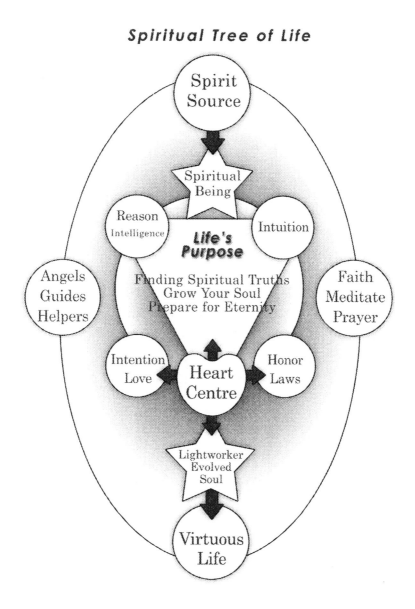

Chapter 13

Find Your True Potential through Adversity, Problems and Suffering

Adversity cause some men to break; others to break records.
William Arthur Ward

Your purpose is not to avoid life's problems. Although this truth is painful, difficult and uncomfortable to accept, you can only grow and develop your spirit when you go through rough and difficult times. While you are experiencing adversity, it is hard for you to accept that the suffering is good for you. When life seems unfair, embrace the blessing. Sometimes, even evolved souls experience doubt while they are going through unpleasant tragedies. Think of Jesus while he was praying before his crucifixion. We have programmed our minds that we are *human beings* and that we have human limitations, and through our ignorance, we focus on this illusion. Sometimes we use this convenient excuse of being human to create a diversion to tackle our problems and to overcome them. We also use it as an excuse to take accountability for our actions. When we are in control of our being we choose to focus on the fact that we are a *spiritual being* first that can overcome all problems, and achieve whatever we desire. Only when you are able to grasp and obtain this accurate perspective, will you be able to learn life's lessons and you will be able to equip your soul. You are not supposed to avoid life's problems; you have to learn how to face up to your problems and how to conquer them. You have to emerge as a stronger person after experiencing the problem. No soul will have to experience any problem that is beyond its strength or that which you incapable of solving. Most often, you are unaware of your greatness, which is within. You can only find this greatness after you have made a great sacrifice by tearing down and then starting to build up again. We are on earth to go through tests and challenges. We have all the strengths and weaknesses within us, and only we can choose on which one we are going to place our focus. When you are born, you are not perfect, except for the tiny divine spark, which is within you. This divine spark is your undeveloped perfection, which is within your soul. As you develop and manifest each aspect of your being, your perception of this development is a consistent struggle for development, unfoldment, growth and attainment towards self-mastery. You always act on your free will, which rules your circumstances, your character and your nature. Your choices will determine how you will proceed forward. Look again at Fig.1 where we have discussed your individual purpose in life. You get crossroads on which you act through making a choice on which road you will follow. The outcome of your choice on the way forward, results into a consequence. You are always in charge as to which way you will go after you have arrived at a certain point at the crossroads of your own destiny. You have to go through tests repeatedly, to prepare yourself for eternity while you are on earth. The more talents and gifts you have will result in a greater responsibility and trials that you have to go through. Rest assured that your soul will not have to go through a challenge or test until it is spiritually ready, meaning that you will not have to go through any experience before you are ready. The divine laws are perfect, only when you are ready and evolved enough for the difficulty that you have to experience will it cross your path. You learn your greatest lessons on earth through experiencing grief, sorrow, sickness and suffering. When your soul experiences grief and it touches the fiber of your being, it enables your soul to awaken thus; you discover the greatness of your soul, through conquering the difficulty. Think back to our silversmith. You cannot get the gold of your spirit to emerge until you have purified and refined it under the hot flames, you can only accomplish the purification through sorrow and hardship.

Do not complain during difficult times. Embrace the blessing because difficulty and hardship is good for your soul. You may not enjoy the experience while you are going through it, but you will look back in hindsight and you will rejoice for the opportunities that enabled you to extract the gold within you. Through the hard lessons, we are able to attain the things, which are worth attaining, such as spiritual growth. The laws are always working through the difficult and the pleasant times. You cannot judge your Creator, or the universe or yourself. Place your trust in your Creator and have the certainty that He always balances the scales. Sometimes what you perceive as a disaster is in fact a victory, and sometimes when you think you have accomplished triumph, it is a disaster. Be consciously aware that your Creator rules through love and wisdom, and that it is through the fire that one forms steel. Be honest with yourself, when do you truly call on your Creator? Most of the time, it is when you feel that you are at wits' end and when you are in the hour of difficulty. Then, either consciously because you know, or unconsciously, because you see no other way out, you call upon your original, undeveloped and dormant divinity. When you understand the spiritual reality that there is only one way that your soul can find itself, through what you perceive as difficulties, then you are able to see and understand your Creators' divine plan. You have now awakened to the reality, that each one of us has received just the right amount of free will, and as we evolve, we learn how to prudently apply our free will. The higher you climb on the spiritual ladder, the more you can exercise your free will. You understand now that your spirit is superior to your physical body and that you can accomplish whatever you desire because the divine spark is within you.

The right-minded man must care more for the truth than for what other people think. Aristotle

You have now discovered one of the greatest secrets of life.

Please read the following statement three times and then meditate on it: *Spiritual attainment is a complex, difficult and lonely path.* As you move along your path, you will leave the familiar landmarks and signposts behind, venturing into the unknown will result into the perception that you are all alone. Your quest for spiritual attainment is a lonely quest but the divine unseen powers always accompany you. Your fate and destiny is that of the pilgrim who walks the lonely and unfamiliar path. Be steadfast and persevere for you have the knowledge and faith that God accompanies you. Your Creator will test you repeatedly to measure if you are true, honest and pure in your intentions and if you are enthusiastic to share your knowledge. Have the certainty in your heart that just as there is justice for all the selfish and unkind acts of earthy life; that equally the compensation for those who record the lonely path of the spirit and that your intention is to increase spiritual awareness that it will result into inner confidence and divine approval and protection. Every individual has to earn the greatest- and most difficult prizes, themselves!

You have the Creators' guarantee that through serving Him and by giving service that you have attracted your departed loved ones to assist and guide you with unconditional love. The most affirming fact and certainty is that God's' Angels, the Great Shining Ones, which He has given custody of (through safekeeping you), and who have protected you from the day of your birth, that they truly and consistently act as guides and as your divine helpers. Now, ponder on the following statement: *You may feel that the path is lonely and that God has forgotten you when you have to tread the tough and demanding unfamiliar curves all by yourself.* The facts are: you are not alone. God safeguards you with His protective shield, which is around you to ensure that you will get through your difficulty with victory. Your Creators' love is your sanctuary, the strength of your spirit is your refuge and the wisdom of your spirit is your haven! God always encircles you with his loving arms and His profound guidance even if you cannot see it. The people on earth may fail you but on the contrary, God will never neglect or fail you!

We can learn from one another and we can make life a little easier when we help someone who experiences pain, anguish and sorrow. Learn to put your focus on someone else instead of focusing on your own problems. When you look at others, you may see that your problem is small compared to their challenges. I got the following quotation from a hospital in Hermanus, close to Cape Town in South Africa. They have a remembrance wall on cancer patients of all ages. Kashmira Maharajh, an Acute Lymphoblastic Leucaemia (leukemia) patient was only seven years old when he spoke the following words of wisdom: *When you need to choose between two paths, do not choose the easy one. That will lead you away from your destination. Even worse, do not remain indecisive and remain where you are. That will lead you nowhere.* K. Maharajh

Chapter 14

Finding Spiritual Truth will Result in Giving Love and Service

One of the greatest sources of energy and motivation is feeling compassionate for others; it awakens your true desire to be of service and make a difference.

J. Gray

When you realize the purpose of life, it will give you an idea of how the whole system works and it will give you guidance on how you can be an honest and devoted ministrant to your Creator. The key is to give love and service to your Creator, humanity, the animal kingdom and the environment. *The best way to find yourself is to lose yourself in the service of others* Gandhi. My seven year old, Serena Elizabeth will affirm: Smile and give love, kisses, hugs and help to your *species*. You can perform no task or service, which will give you the equivalent satisfaction as when you help others. When you help someone the joy that you receive back is priceless. No source of pleasure can match the feeling as when you uplift and help others. Millions of individuals are lost and troubled in today's world. It is your responsibility, to search for individuals, who need your help and comfort. You can show them the way and affirm that they are part of God's divine plan, and His arms of infinite love surround them. Share with them the fact that they have to realize that God will never neglect or forget them. The most important task that you can accomplish is to help a person to find himself and to find peace and serenity within. If you can help one lonely, sad person out of the darkness into the light, you have given a profound service to your Creator. Our whole purpose in life is to awaken firstly our own souls to prepare for eternity, and secondly to awaken the sleeping, undeveloped souls to the reality of their existence. Our world has many sleepwalkers who go through the day's activities dreaming. You have accomplished a great task when an individual is not aware of the realities of life (that he is a subdivision of God), and you help the individual to discover and revive his divine flame. We are fulfilling our purpose when we help humanity towards enlightenment; therefore we are serving the greatest power of the cosmos.

The supreme purpose of your life is to unfold your spirit. You have to give attention to the requirements of your eternal nature. This means that you will focus on the things that will enrich your spirit. It means that you need to love yourself and others and that you need to live in harmony with *your species*. When you give assistance and help, you enrich and grow your spirit. You can help and guide people, but you cannot convert people to adapt   to your thinking. You cannot change individuals, they have to change themselves. When the person is ready and prepared, he will be able to understand and he will be able to receive the spiritual realities. This depends on his level of growth; only when his soul is ready, will he be able to accept the truth; which is the true revelation. People, who do not understand, are simply not spiritually ready. Always share knowledge with compassion, love and grace, and try to do your best. Be a living example and shine your divine light through living your talk. Your intentions must always be pure and not to look for applause and approval from the physical world. Never act on what you can gain in return, give assistance through unconditional selfless love. When you act through your heart, you receive in return the reward of joy. Your intentions must be authentic to fulfill your purpose for which you were born, and you must have no regrets that you have not completed your tasks. You have to convey clarification and enlightenment to the children of the Creator. When you share spiritual truths, you illuminate and help to heal the world and in return, Shekinah's divine protection hovers over you. This is the spiritual law.

You cannot live the lives of others, even though you love them dearly. You can only take complete responsibility for your life, which means that everything you see, hear, taste, touch or in any way experience is your responsibility. Only you are responsible for your actions, you are not responsible for the actions that others performed. You have a lifetime to ensure that you live in harmony with your actions, thoughts, words, dreams, desires and aspirations according to the knowledge that you have received from your Creator. You can also not behave in a way that contradicts the knowledge that you have received on your path so far. When you behave wrongly and you are aware of it, you will pay a greater price than those who behave immorally, and sinfully without knowing, because they are ignorant. You have to realize that this is the perfect spiritual law in action. On the other hand, when you touch a soul and you are uplifting and helping it, you are now fulfilling your divine purpose, which results in soul-growth. You have to earn self-realization, there are no short cuts or easy ways. The joy that you receive in return is that you are fulfilling the purpose of your being and your Creators' power is flowing through you. Through self-realization, you know that you belong to eternity and that this life is only temporary, for you are preparing your soul for eternity. The only way for you to receive your Creators' stamp of approval is to give assistance, help and love to *your species*! You have to embrace the honor that God choose you to give service to your fellows and to be able to express His great love through making a difference to someone.

Chapter 15

Have Faith

Now faith is the substance of things hoped for, the evidence
of things not seen.
Hebrews 11.1

A fundamental truth is that your Creator will never quit on you. I strongly recommend that you also read the complete chapter on faith, Hebrews 11.1-40

To enhance your understanding of faith, make a date with yourself today and purchase the DVD *Faith like Potatoes* - www.faithlikepotatoes.com - this is an inspiring and true story of a farmer Angus Buchan's moving journey who like his potatoes, grows his faith, unseen until the harvest. *The seed for a great miracle lies not in difficulty, but impossibility.* A Buchan

Trust in the Lord with all thine heart; and learn not unto thine own understanding. Proverbs 3:5

Now that you have a true perspective and focus on your life, you know that you are a survivor. You are truly aware that your soul is immortal. You have the wisdom that you are able to attract the right vibrations and divine strength whenever you need it. You know that you have to stand up for yourself and that there is no need to feel inadequate when you experience problems. The good and the other are learning phases to assist you in accomplishing self-mastery. You know that God and His Angels are protecting you. However, even now, you have to progress, which means that you will get new, greater challenges that you have to overcome and master.

Our spirit weakens when we experience daily conflicts and then our circumstances seem to be insurmountable. When our spirit is weak, our troubles seem to be more powerful and overwhelming. When you have too many matters to address at once, the results will be that of a downward spiral. You will experience moments and effects of discourse and dissatisfaction. It is hard to remember and to focus on spiritual truths while you are experiencing tremendous and severe unhappiness and sadness. For all the works, mechanisms, processes and technicalities to work, you have to begin with the core (focus and open your heart center) then change your thinking process. You have to stand your ground firmly and confidently to be able to change your thought processes for all the works and mechanics to work in synchronization and in harmony. You have to focus on your thoughts and affirm a message that will engage and enhance your level of attainment while you are struggling with daily difficulties. You have to readjust yourself and consciously feed your soul with the fact that your spirit is the master over your physical body and unwanted circumstances. Your focus has to be on the truth that you are a tiny part of God and that you have the divine spark within you.

You have to be able to balance and align yourself with your purest of thoughts, and you have to activate them into a measurement that will engage many new vibrations of action by which you will be able to tackle and turn into a better and positive light. This brings us back to aligning your chakras, which help to distribute energy for your physical, emotional, mental and spiritual functions. When your chakras are in perfect balance, your state of consciousness gives you a feeling of harmony, total bliss, contentment and tranquility. Your new mindset and balanced chakras will assist you in finding feelings such as harmony, satisfaction and contentment within. Through spiritual, mental, emotional and physical balance, you will experience total acceptance and a feeling of worth, which will allow even the most distressed person to release unwanted and unwelcome feelings. Acceptance of *the self* and self-love are the starting points of all healing and inner harmony. You have to gently embrace yourself with self-acceptance. Turn to God when you are ready to help you to balance all aspects of your being. You only have to accept His love and assistance graciously. Use sacred sounds, whether as prayer, song, music, chants or invocations whenever you are feeling down. These different forms of sound are a fundamental force, which permeates and infuses every aspect of creation; it can help you to uplift your spirit instantaneously. Shift your perspective to the divine sphere when you experience feelings such as conflict, imbalance or difficulty. When you listen to uplifting music it can help you to alter your physical energies, eases pain and restores homeostasis to physiological and psycho-logical states. Enjoy your new applications in your achievement of altered states of your consciousness, through the healing and uplifting effect of music, prayer, song and chants.

A fundamental spiritual truth is that your Creator will never quit on you.

The following story continuously traveled the world to give inspiration and hope:

Throughout generations, they have told the story and they have shared it with the next generation. Each generation honored the safekeeping and circulation of this uplifting message. The purpose is to give hope and enlightenment worldwide. It will help you to have a balanced lifestyle, and it will help you to be able to continuously deal with your daily challenges.

One day I decided to quit... I quit my job, my relationship, and my spirituality. I wanted to quit my life. I went to the woods to have one final talk with God. God, I said: Can you give me one good reason not to quit? God's answer surprised me:

Look around, He said: Do you see the fern and the bamboo? Yes, I replied. When I planted the fern and the bamboo seeds, I took very good care of them. I gave them light and I gave them water. The fern quickly responded and grew from the earth. Its brilliant green lusciously covered the floor. Yet, nothing came from the bamboo seed. However, I did not quit on the bamboo. In the second year, the fern grew even more vibrant and plentiful. Again, nothing came from the bamboo seed. But still, I did not quit on the bamboo. He said: During the third year there was still not anything from the bamboo seed. Nevertheless, I would not quit. In year four, again, there was nothing from the bamboo seed. Yet, I would not quit. He said:

Then in the fifth year a tiny sprout emerged from the earth. Compared to the fern it was seemingly small and insignificant. However, just six months later the bamboo rose to over a 100 feet tall. It had spent the last five years growing its roots. Those roots made it strong and gave it what it needed to survive. I would never give any of my creations a challenge that it could not handle and conquer. He told me.

Are you aware my child, that all this time you have been struggling, you have actually been growing your roots?

I would not quit on the bamboo. I will certainly, never quit on you. Never compare yourself to others. He said. The bamboo had a different purpose than the fern. Yet they both make the forest beautiful.

Your time will come, God said to me. You will rise high. How high should I rise? I asked. How high will the bamboo rise? He asked in return. As high as it can? I questioned?

Yes, He said, give me glory by rising as high as you can.

So, always place your faith in God. Keep shining; always do the best that you can! – Author Unknown

So much to do – so little time left

You can make the comparison that through your adversities you have grow your roots. By growing your roots, it results into preparing your soul for eternity. You know that you have only a certain time span on this planet. You may think you have forever but the fact is that you have little time left. How old are you? Brace yourself for the next paradigm shock: Work out the amount of days that you have on earth and you will think differently about how much time you have. Let me give you an example. *The average person lives (from birth to death) for approximately 70 years. Now take the 70 years x 365 days in a year = 25,550 days on earth.* Now, think again about how much time you have – I hope you have changed your perspective. Take your age and work it out for yourself. If you are at present 40 years of age, you only have 10,950 days left on this planet. You have already spent 14,600 days on earth (if you live until the age of 70) take 25,550 – 14,600 = 10,950 days that you have left in which you have to live your life, accomplish all your tasks and dreams, and emerge your soul. Now change your mindset. Spend your precious time wisely! Do not attach yourself to the unimportant and insignificant human and worldly standards such as wealth, the craving for high corporate positions, authority and power and material possessions. The great master taught us that when you die, you will not be in a position to take your earthly possessions or your 'important' title with you. Do not cast your pearls in front of the pigs; this is a profound wisdom from the bible. Through your awakening and by expanding you knowledge and talents (your pearls) you have received a blessing, it is your responsibility to further expand, nurture and share this knowledge.

No one is saying that you have to live a life of poverty. You need to live a balanced life and your focus and priorities should be on spiritual attainment. There is enough abundance in the world for all of us. Materialism must not be your master, and you cannot measure success according to your materialistic possessions. *Seek first His kingdom and His righteousness, and all these things shall be yours as well.* Matthew 6.33. I have read somewhere that there is enough money in the world that every single person on earth can be a millionaire. God expects you to develop all your talents, skills and strengths so that they bear fruit, which will attract prosperity into your life. It is your responsibility to balance your mind, body and soul. The absence of balance and when you focus on the wrong things such as acquisitions will result in life's destruction, meaninglessness, unhappiness and emptiness. Prosperity will find you when you first focus on God, and when you stand your ground through clear and calm actions. You have to be appreciative, prudent, responsible and thankful. You have to invest in yourself, your talents, your skills and experiences, which will open the right doors for you. Through living a balanced and virtuous life, God will in return shower you with His love and blessings.

This brings us to the question that you have to ask yourself: When you help someone, do you do it with unconditional love, affection, compassion and devotion? Are your intentions pure? When you can answer yes to this question your have evolved your character and the reward is the eternal guarantee and promise, which is registered on your soul. When you know within your heart and soul that you have truly provided the greatest help you can give, then indeed you have developed your supremacies to their peak and you have done your best. This will result in receiving God's seal of approval, and you have matured your soul to a higher level.

No seemingly difficult problem or situation is too big for your Creator to give you guidance and to help you. If you think you have problems, think back to Jonah, which called on God from inside the belly of a huge whale. *In my distress I cried to the LORD and He answered me, from the depths I called, and Lord, You heard me!* Jonah 2.2. The only responsibility you have when you are going through a difficult time is to call out to God and to surrender and release yourself and your problem into His arms of infinite love. Through your Creator's grace, you can expect a miracle after experiencing hard times.

Chapter 16

Sharing Knowledge - Be a Teacher and a Lightworker

Treat people as if they were what they ought to be and you help them to become what they are capable of being.
Goethe

A teacher of God is anyone who chooses to be one, choose to be a Lightworker! It is easy to arrange a meeting or workshops and brainstorm sessions of what we should be doing and then never do anything about it. We have to take action and do something that will make a difference in our life as well as someone else's. People will never know what they can accomplish if they do nothing.

Now that we are aware that we only have little time left on earth, we need to really put our focus where we can make the most significant difference. Sharing your knowledge and helping individuals (both old and young) must be first nature to you. We are now going to focus on our children, we are not going to discuss the obvious tuition in all the sciences and subjects that will assist the child to develop and cultivate his mind. They are part of the natural development that a child has to accomplish. Children have to learn about the natural events and occurrences of life. To me the greatest difference that one can make is to teach our children spiritual truths. They are the ones that have to manage our planet when we move on to the next plane. It is our responsibility to remove all the misconceptions from our past and we have to open the road for our children, which will result in a smoother passage for them.

Through receiving truths, it will put an end to poverty,

ignorance and sorrow, and our children can live our dream of having peace and harmony on earth. Our world longs for repair. We have millions of unprivileged individuals who fear the next day when the sun will rise. We need to spread and broaden the reality and truth that all the people in the world are parts of one another, and that they are all part of the supreme force, their Creator. When God looks at us, He sees all His children, His divine spirit flows through all human beings, which makes all of us equal in God's eyes. We are all equal as far as our natures are concerned. You will achieve greatness when; you as a Lightworker who is more advanced in character, in development, in growth and in understanding; attempt to share what you possess with those who lack these possessions. It is your responsibility to share your wisdom. Evolved souls can be any race, color or position, and evolved souls do not see color, race or designation and religion. When you look through your spiritual eyes, you see God's divine children. We have to teach the natural law of cause and effect (regarding service to anyone that needs help) to all children on earth. As they give help, it will result in applying the law, and as the law has to fulfill itself, in return they themselves will receive help. It is not a bribe or a reward; it is once again the perfect law in operation. True intentions from the heart will attract the right vibrations in return. An important fact that we need to share with our children is that of religious education. Our children of today are the men and women of tomorrow and of the future. We need to prepare our children for the life that lies ahead after they have completed their school education. They need to be ready and equipped with the necessary knowledge to be prepared to face their tasks as balanced citizens and adults. The fundamental and essential responsibility that we have is to teach our children that they are all citizens of the world. We need to share knowledge and wisdom in such a way that it will give guidance and enables our children to live in harmony within their immediate surroundings and within the greater world. In simpler terms, true education means that we have to share exact and accurate instructions with our children on all the natural laws of the universe. We need to share with them from the earliest age possible, that they have various senses, gifts, talents, powers and abilities. We have to teach our children how to develop and unfold all these faculties to their greatest potential. When all these gifts work in harmony and when they develop their gifts to their fullest potential, our children will be able to use their abilities to help themselves and to help the world around them. Through attaining spiritual knowledge, our children will be able to put an end to wars based on religion, color and race. There will be no need for conflicts for their focus will be on enhancing the spirit within themselves and they will focus on spiritual matters. They will understand one another and they will share the world in harmony. With knowledge and wisdom, all obstructions, barriers and problems will fall away that creates conflict. The children are the future and we have to help them to expand their minds and souls. We have to feed their souls with spiritual truths.

Children's minds are soft and impressionable. A young child, does not judge for the plain reason that he or she has no instinctive way or indication of judgment. Children are pure open-minded and susceptible. Youngsters are receptive and they do not weigh up whether the statements, which you teach, are true, false, or if they contain only a portion of truth. The mind of a child is very genuine and pliable and, being trustworthy, a young child will accept whatever you propose and suggest as truths. Whatever teaching you put forward during the very early ages of a child's upbringing will not be questioned by the child for the child is very acceptable at this age. You have a tremendous responsibility towards any child, you are dealing with very precious and very delicate material, and you are helping the child to form impressions and beliefs that will become part of the child's integral and essential being. You are embedding images, feeling, teachings and impressions onto the child's subconscious mind, which will have an effect on the child for the rest of his earthy life. These images will have a coloring effect on the child in later life. Ask yourself the following question: *How do you view the world?* Do you see the world in color or black and white? When you are well-balanced, positive, optimistic, adventurous, joyous, happy and open-minded you see color; when you are always having some crises, are negative, depressed, judgmental, you are pessimistic, feeling sorry for yourself, you demand that the world owes you and you always have issues, you see black and white. When you deliberately instill principles, which are false, for whatever reason, you are guilty of extremely serious damage to the future of society and the human race. The Inca Wisdom is full of profound sayings and life wisdoms such as that a light hand will guide and a heavy hand will destroy. Do you guide or do you enforce your teachings? Then there is the issue of ignorance: Men and women who are ignorant of the child's potentialities and adults, who are unfamiliar with the spiritual realities, will as a consequence be unable to teach the child truths about his own being and his own nature. Ignorant adults will also be unable to teach the child about his/her relationship and divine link with the Creator and God's overall divine plan, this will result in the child being handicapped, meaning the child will have a backward position. Handicap in this context means that the child has limited knowledge and thus will start his progress and go through the rest of his life as if he is already in 'arrears'. Therefore, it is your responsibility as Lightworker and advanced soul to take it upon yourself to teach ignorant adults as well as children about spiritual truths. A part of any child's divine birthright is to be able to go through life as fully equipped and geared with knowledge and wisdom as God intended to. The essence of all education is freedom, which means that the child can make his own choices and exercise his free will with a lack of restrictions. We are all spiritual beings; our essence is that part of us which is the tiny part of our Creator. Through this essential part of a child's being he has the right to live with all the benefits that freedom offers him. Religion plays a primal part in the education of a child; religion must therefore offer the child guidance to his soul. Through this guidance, the child must be able to face and conquer all life's battles. The traditional definition for religion includes the belief system, faith, creeds, dogma and religious convictions. When I use the word religion, I want you to think about service and touching souls. I want you to think about a belief system that shares spiritual truths, which will not contradict, restrict, oppose, disagree or say the opposite of God's natural eternal laws and that will uplift and expand the soul of a young child. This will help the young child to rise above any earthly problem or difficulty, when you gear a child with true spiritual knowledge, he will be able to rely on spirit and he will not focus on material problems. It is thus your responsibility to guide the child to find authentic spiritual truths. The basis of your teaching must not support your desires or loyalty to ancient myth and fable. The origin, center and foundation of your teachings must represent God's authentic spiritual truths, thus the sharing of the Divine unchangeable supreme and perfect natural laws. Think back to our bamboo story. You have to help the young child and feed its roots with solid and true spiritual nutrition, vitamins and love. The child has to be able to grow into a formidable strong, straight and well-built tree or bamboo, meaning a well-balanced adult. When you 'feed' the child wrong nutrition through your teachings, you will tamper with the child's roots and his integral being, this will result in holding back, slowing down or even retarding the child's growing. We have a responsibility, and through the perfect laws, we are accountable. You have to think before you act; the truth about our religions today is that all the different religions possess only a part of the truths. None of the religions possesses the whole truth and throughout the ages, the information has become vague and imprecise. The creedsmen who formulated the religious doctrine intentions were to have control and power over all people. They insisted that all individuals followed the traditional statements and beliefs. You should now have a clear understanding why it is cardinal to use your own reason before you blindly accept that which someone taught you while you did not judge the content yourself during your early vulnerable years of upbringing. For the same reason, you should teach the child that true religion is service, and to live an honest life filled with integrity and unselfish desires. The greatest service that he can perform is to live a virtuous life, which enhances and develops his divine light within to his fullest potential. He needs to be true to his Creator because he is a tiny part of his Creator. It is natural and first nature for children to trust their inner wisdom and intuition. For this reason it is very easy to explain the Creator, the power of all life to them. Show them the divine artwork of nature, which is God's perfect canvas. Show the children the lovely flickering stars; they are the diamonds in the sky and the lovely silver-white moon, which accompanies the stars. Point to them the glory of the sun, which warms and illuminates the world. Show them the trickling stream, the mighty ocean, the colorful sand dunes, puffy clouds, abundant flowers, huge forests and a tiny baby. Teach them to respect all creatures such as tiny insects and all wildlife. After you have shown them God's work of art, you can share with them that the divine entity they call God, is the supreme mind behind the creation of the lovely universe.

Chapter 17

When Are You a True Lightworker?

We all need four or five people in our lives whose faces light up when
we walk into the room.
J. Lair

You are a Lightworker when you demonstrate God's love, grace and compassion everywhere. You have to show people through your own way of living that you represent your Creator. You need to inspire, uplift, nurture, love and truly help people who are suffering. It is through your physical actions, (what you are doing to make a difference) and when you help someone that you register on your soul (psychic faculty), your soul- growth (spirit). A Lightworker will not tolerate wickedness, injustice, abusive behavior, unfairness, discrimination, prejudice, poverty, sickness, starvation and unemployment. You have to declare war on all the unfairness in the physical word and you need to do your utmost best to help someone under any of the above circumstances whenever you can. The great master showed us through his example that we have to look for people who need our help; we need to search the main roads as well as the side streets for people in distress. You have to go to them! You need to be similar to a centre of light, which not only feeds their souls but their physical starving bodies as well. Poor people need clothes, bread, shelter and the necessities of life and not only words of wisdom. They need to survive to be able to see the sunlight the next day. When you help someone, the person has to experience God's unconditional love through your actions. True Lightworkers do things, they take action, they make a difference – they are the change agents who make life a little easier for those who struggle! God handpicked all His Lightworkers, He called many but only a few succeed in seeing the challenge through. Choose to be a true Lightworker and make your Creator proud! Always be consistent. You have to be a Lightworker in your personal capacity as well as in your professional capacity.

Gandhi defined the roots of violence as follows: *Wealth without work, pleasure without conscience, knowledge without character, commerce without morality, science without humanity, worship without sacrifice and politics without principles.* Your name doesn't have to be a rich or famous celebrity to make a difference in the word. When you are fortunate to be in a high position and you have power over directives and company policies, you can make a great difference in the corporate world as well as worldwide. Lightworkers can be God's strategic change agents and by leading your company with integrity and by implementing virtues you can show the way to others. Be the change that you want to see in the world through tolerance, patience and long-term goals. Intolerance betrays want of faith in one's cause. Stop chasing materialism, selfishness and greed, earth provides enough to satisfy every man's need. Companies can invest in employees and projects dedicated to upliftment of sorrow, poverty and ignorance. You can really change the world and make a difference when you care enough and you can still show a positive profit without loosing anything. You may attract more contracts and clients because you are fair and virtuous. The benefit to you is that you will feel good, you will give service and you will grow your soul.

Part III

Be kinder than necessary because everyone you meet is fighting some kind of battle.
Unknown

Chapter 18

Virtuous Living - Connecting Matter and Spirit

One day I said to GOD -
I'm going to search
For the meaning to my existence
I'm going to find the talent within me
Then develop it to the best of my ability
And I'm going to make the most of this life
That I have been given
And I'm going to do this
Without infringing upon anyone else's
Opportunity to do the same
And GOD replied
'I couldn't ask for anything more'.
Benjamin Franklin (1790)
Autobiography of Benjamin Franklin,
Books, Inc. Publishers, New York.

What is a Virtuous Circle and what is Virtue?

The Oxford Dictionary describes a Virtuous Circle as a beneficial recurring cycle of cause and effect. This explanation merges perfectly with the theme of our book and we have discussed the supreme natural law of cause and effect in detail within part one and two. We have to be able to apply virtuous behavior daily to grow our souls and to master the self.

The Webster enhances this true description and defines virtue as a moral practice or action. This highlights the supreme, perfect law once again. When you practice morality, you conform to a standard of right, which is the divine law or highest good. Think about what we a saying, take a minute… when we conform, we obey the rules and we do the accepted things, we honor and obey our Creators' laws - you have to agree, this is profound insight! When you live a virtuous life you have accomplished moral excellence, which means your character's essence is built on integrity, honesty, rectitude, ethics and decent behavior. In other words, you are honoring God's divine, natural, supreme laws. Through virtuous living, you live a life of the highest good to all including yourself, humanity, the animal kingdom and the environment. Compromising your integrity for whatever reason is not an option. You obey the ultimate rules, which are the divine laws! When you live a virtuous life, you have to implement the following guidelines, which will result into excellence.

Virtue is not to be considered in the light of mere innocence, or abstaining from harm, but as the exertion of our faculties in doing good. Joseph Butler, Philanthropis, Philosopher and Historian, 1692 O.S. – 1752

The next qualities will give you an indication of what you should be focusing on to be able to live a virtuous life. You have to aspire to obtain morale excellence, goodness and uprightness, which consist of decency, honesty, morality and respectability. When you are virtuous, you possess and show moral rectitude, which means you are living a life of righteousness (virtue). Your actions are thus steadfast and you follow moral and ethical principles. Virtue is its own reward, as the basis of wisdom is the knowledge of good that makes one act in accordance with the good. Your actions will reflect a particular moral excellence. When you always act through compassion, people will acknowledge you through (the very virtue of compassion). Virtue is a habit, which involves the choice of excellence in your behavior. When you realize that you have imperfections or shortcomings, you will choose through exercising virtue, that you will improve on your shortcomings. Your actions will portray grace, mercy and integrity. Mercy is a generous, compassionate good wish, an increase of a feeling of love for others. Abraham Lincoln described mercy as *Malice towards none with charity for all*. When you live a virtuous life you have to act with goodwill, kindness and you have to withhold punishment and suffering from all which crosses your path.

'Father of light and life, thou Good Supreme!
O teach me what is good; teach me Thyself!
Save me from folly, vanity, and vice,
From every low pursuit; and fill my soul
With knowledge, conscious peace, and virtue pure;
Sacred, substantial, never-fading bliss!
Benjamin Franklin-1790

Chapter 19

The Advocates of Virtue

Aliud est theoria, aliud est practica – One thing is theory, another thing is practice.
Roman Saying

One of the greatest passions throughout the ages was to encourage and inspire every member of society to instill virtuous astuteness and wisdom into their daily lives. For this reason 'religion' was initially born. When we go back to the earliest writings of civilization, it shows that those early fundamental principals were rooted to encourage and train people that deep-seated principals were essential and that they will lead, when you practice them, to a peaceful, harmonious and productive society. Without a set of firm well-developed behavioral rules, people are out of balance and they rule on anarchy and chaos, which results into bloodshed and war, destruction, selfishness and stealing for survival. When lawlessness rules, we have a tendency to live for the moment and we thrive only on our physical most basic desires. Our most natural inclination and preference, like the animals, will be that our basic instinct will control and have power over us. We have said earlier that the truly great individuals are those who can exercise self-control and who can manage their physical desires. These times are the times when we learn most about life, our strengths and weaknesses and through accomplishing self-mastery; we achieve the award of true virtue. *Mankind differs from the animals only by a little, and most people throw that away.* Confucius

The virtues that we would like to cultivate and reward in individuals today, resulted from the true ancient written and spoken wisdoms of individuals such as Plato, Confucius, Aristotle, Buddha, Mohammed, and The Master - Jesus of Nazareth, as well as from extracts of the scriptures that they have produced or quoted as gurus of virtues.

When we study the original historical teachings, there are four cardinal virtues, which are prudence, temperance, fortitude and justice. Then there are three heavenly graces - faith, hope and charity (love). The center or capital virtues are humility, liberality, brotherly love, meekness, chastity, temperance and diligence. The center (main) sins, sometimes revered to as *the seven deadly sins*, are pride, avarice (greed), envy, wrath, lust, gluttony and sloth. An interesting thought, there are seven core values, and seven core sins. Our basic essential periods of human life, consists of seven-year cycles of life. The biblical scripture teaches us that God created earth in seven days. We also have seven *contrary* virtues that we discuss later. Now ponder on the thought and the synchronicity of the number seven.

We can trace back the first four virtues (*prudence, temperance, fortitude and justice*) and the seven deadly sins (*pride, avarice (greed), envy, wrath, lust, gluttony and sloth*) to the Greek philosophers and Christian theologians who readily adopted them, arguing that they were applicable to all humans thus Christian and otherwise. The final three virtues (*chastity, temperance and diligence*) developed out of the Christian theological work, but in particular from the writings of Paul in the New Testament of the Bible.

There are also seven *contrary* virtues: Humility, kindness, abstinence, chastity, patience, generosity and diligence. We call them *contrary* because each one stands in direct opposition to one of the seven deadly sins. The essence of the belief or principal is that through your conscious attempt to cultivate and develop these virtues, they will help you to avoid their contrary sins. Through understanding, the *contrary* virtues you can act accordingly. Humility versus pride, kindness versus envy, abstinence versus gluttony, chastity versus lust, patience versus anger, generosity versus greed, and diligence versus sloth.

Confucius or 'Master Kung'

The strength of a nation derives from the integrity of the home. Confucius

Confucius a Chinese thinker and social philosopher lived 551-479 years before Jesus Christ in what we today call and know as China. It was his true passion to teach humans about the qualities of being good. His wisdom conveyed that we have to rule by means of moral example rather than by force and violence. Confucius said that a ruler who had to resort to force had already failed as a ruler: *Your job is to govern, not to kill.* Confucius was the inventor of the golden rule: *Do not unto others what you would not have them do unto you.* Through original writings which were recorded, they have extracted the following statement: Confucius demanded that his pupils be *quick in apprehension, clear in discernment of, far-reaching intelligences and all-embracing knowledge, fitted to exercise rule, magnanimous, fitted to exercise forbearance.* They had to learn *gravity, earnestness, faithfulness, kindness and a reverent attention to business.* (Reader's Digest Great Lives, Great Deeds, Max Eastman, 'The Wisdom of Confucius', 1965: 132). Confucius placed great emphasis on sincerity and said that to travel *the path of truth* there must be no self-deception. He is recognized and worshipped for his teachings of the pure, high, temperate and simple art of living and the virtue of the family as a unit of love.

Confucius's – Most famous and well known sayings:

- *Virtue is not left to stand alone. He who practices it will have.*
- *To be able under all circumstances to practice five things constitutes perfect virtue; these five things are gravity, generosity of soul, sincerity, earnestness and kindness.*
- *A man should practice what he preaches, but a man should also*

preach what he practices.

- *They must often change, who would be constant in happiness or wisdom.*
- *It is not possible for one to teach others who cannot teach his own family.*
- *The superior man is modest in his speech but exceeds in his actions.*
- *He who merely knows right principles is not equal to him who loves them.*
- *We don't know yet about life, how can we know about death?*
- *Mankind differs from the animals only by a little, and most people throw that away.*
- *If you enjoy what you do, you'll never work another day in your life.*
- *It is only the wisest and the very stupidest who cannot change.*
- *I hear and I forget. I see and I remember. I do and I understand.*
- *Golden Rule: Do not unto others what you would not have them do unto you.*

Confucius said, (the good man) does not grieve that other people do not recognize his merits. His only anxiety is lest he should fail to recognize theirs.

The Buddha or 'The Enlightened One'

There are only two mistakes one can make along the road to truth; not going all the way, and not starting.
Buddha

The Buddha or *The Enlightened One*, who also lived 500 years before Jesus Christ, similarly made a great contribution to our virtue intelligence. His truest interest/passion was to teach people a noble and happy way of living and dying in the present world. He believed that peace and perfect happiness sprang from liberating the mind from superstition, from strict disciplining of the will, from flooding the world with love and being humble (1bid: 132). His eightfold path to salvation reads like this:

- *Blessed are they who know, and whose knowledge is free from delusion.*
- *Blessed are they who speak what they know in a kindly, open and truthful manner.*
- *Blessed are those whose conduct is peaceful, honest and pure.*
- *Blessed are they who earn their livelihood in a way that brings hurt or danger to no living thing.*
- *Blessed are the tranquil, who cast out ill will, pride, self-righteousness, and put in their place love, pity and sympathy.*
- *Blessed are ye when ye direct your efforts to self-training and self-control.*
- *Blessed beyond measure, when ye are by this means unwrapped from the limitations of selfhood.*
- *And blessed, finally are they who find rapture in contemplating what is deeply and really true about this world and our life in it.*

According to Buddha's teachings, people who follow this path of salvation will reach *Nirvana* – the ideal state of peace and happiness. His teachings have guided the thoughts and behavior of millions of people for more than two thousand years (2508) to be precise. Like all spiritual Lightworkers before Buddha, he taught that we have to seek and find spiritual truth. He advocated that we have to use our reason (one's intelligence) before coming to any conclusion.

Do not believe in anything simply because you have heard it. Do not believe in anything simply because it is spoken and rumored by many. Do not believe in anything simply because it is found written in your religious books. Do not believe in anything merely on the authority of your teachers and elders. Do not believe in traditions because they have been handed down for many generations. But after observation and analysis, when you find that anything agrees with reason and is conducive to the good and benefit of one and all, then accept it and live up to it. Buddha

Jesus of Nazareth 'Greatest Master'

Ego sum veritas – I am the Truth.
The Nazarene- Jesus

Truth is classified as the foundation of all virtues, values and denominations. When Jesus of Nazareth was asked by Pontius Pilot in John 18.37 to state who he was, Jesus replied: *Ego sum veritas – I am the Truth.* For this Roman Governor such an answer was a big surprise, he responded: *Quid est veritas? – What is truth?* Jesus answered: *To this end was I born, and for this cause came I into the world, that I should bear witness unto the truth. Every one that is of the truth heareth my voice.* When we are truthful everybody knows where we stand and where he or she stand with us. There is no ambiguity, vagueness, uncertainty or misunderstanding.

One of our primary goals that we have to accomplish through reading this book is to discover *Truth.* We said earlier that *Truth* is *Truth* and that *Truth* cannot be affected by anybody's opinion of it. We can add to wisdom and knowledge, but *Truth* is consistent, unswerving, and part of God's supreme laws. We also quoted Gandhi, *whenever you have truth it must be given with love, or the message and the messenger will be rejected.* Most of us are unconsciously prejudiced through our upbringing and strict religiously bred traditions; therefore, it is difficult to find *Truth.* Revelation is not unique at any time, in any country, or in any language. You will find truth when you seek like a little child with simplicity for answers. The value of simplicity is beauty. When you find beauty, the asset is splendor, magnificence and exquisiteness. When you truly desire to find only that which is true, your reward will exceed your greatest expectations. Truth is a constant search, therefore; as your soul evolves your mind will respond. Mark 10.15 *Verily I say unto you, whosoever shall not receive the kingdom of God as a little child, he shall not enter therein.*

When we think of revelation the only Source or Origin is God, which is the infinite fountainhead of all revelation. In every age,

God has attempted to overflow the world with the amount of wisdom, inspiration and knowledge that people needed who lived together under specific conditions and suited their needs during that time and age.

Our world today is more complex and interdependent than in earlier times. So are the communities and civilizations. Our national environments and characteristics are different and we have great cultural diversity and racial conflict. God needs to find ways to communicate with us all through our different languages and through the limitations of a diverse population on earth. At present God uses different methods (comparing to the ancient times) to suit different needs. Our population consists of different personalities, different lifestyles, values, thoughts, means and approaches to life and religion. More channels of communication have opened and we have Lightworkers all around the world doing God's humanitarian works by using different methods. These great souls point the way for us to follow, they set a standard which we can standard, and they show us the power of spirit through being a dedicated, selfless servant to God and humanity. True Lightworkers are His dedicated authentic instruments. Take into account that during Jesus' time, the leaders of the churches at that time rejected the power of the spirit and they have accused him of doing the works of the Devil. Once again, those who are suppose to be our greatest supporters because we are doing the works of spirit, are rejecting the same power of the spirit as it operates today, the good news for us is that they do not crucify people any longer because our world has evolved.

We have discussed Confucius and Buddha as advocates of virtue and are now going to discuss Jesus of Nazareth. Jesus came at a time when it was necessary for the revelation of kindness, peace and love towards humanity to illuminate the world.

First, you have to be aware that you should not only turn to the past. You should realize that now, wherever you are, that you have access to the eternal fount of all inspiration – God: God is the spring, the source, the fountain, the true origin and wellspring of all inspiration and truth and we all have direct access to God. The illumination of the world, which Jesus had performed, is the same power of the spirit, which operates in our midst at present.

The word '*Christ*' means '*the anointed*' and there have been many who were anointed; which is to preach good news to the poor. The Nazarene (Jesus) was a person who came to show us the spiritual, psychic and physical life according to the time in which he lived. Luke 10.18 *Why callest, thou me good? There is none good but one, that is, God.* If we through the theological interpretations accept that God took physical form as Jesus, then the whole value of Jesus' life is lost and meaningless. Then the whole point of his mission disappears. Jesus was not the Creator and the Creator is not Jesus. Jesus said *My Father is greater than I* and he spoke of *your God and my God* and he taught us to pray to *Our Father which art in Heaven.* When we read the Bible we should attempt to read it with the understanding of the spirit, spirit will help us to understand and to unlock all the mysteries.

It would have been easy for our Creator to take human form and to live almost a perfect, blameless life. There is no virtue in that. However for a human being, to be born according to the ordinary, natural laws, and to live and show what we all can achieve, that is a worthy example for us all to follow. Jesus went through all the adversities, temptations, pains and experiences that typically cross our paths. He showed us through his example that we can overcome all, we can rise above our realities, and we can conquer death. The whole point of Jesus' mission was to show us how we should and can live. You can read Luke 4, for more detail on Jesus' 40 days of severe temptations and physical adversities; for example, hunger in the desert.

The Bible as we know it today, is not the same as the original scrolls and scriptures on which it was based; the true scrolls and the authentic information are locked up in the Vatican. The records that we have are not free from tampering and are incomplete. We through the ignorance of not knowing, and by only trusting the theological interpretations accept that all the words, which we read in the Bible, are true. We can only say that we *think* that they are true. We cannot say that every word in the Bible on Jesus is in fact his words. Jesus spoke in parables and we also have to take into account that many things in the Bible came from books, which existed a long time before Jesus was born. They are not the original scriptures, therefore; it is cardinal that you trust your own reason. God has implanted your reason within you as a part of God's own reason; your reason will give you guidance on what is true and what is not true. Always keep in mind that the Bible is full of metaphors (images and descriptions) and symbolism (imagery and representations).

When I think of Jesus, I think of a human being who was the most evolved and spiritual being ever to live on earth. Jesus was a messenger of God who came into our world in order to fulfill a mission of God. He fulfilled his mission on earth, but he has not yet fulfilled the rest of his mission, God will give him at the divine time, directions from the spiritual world when he has to fulfill the rest of his mission. Jesus came into our world by fulfilling the natural laws, which God has designed. Jesus was born, he lived and he died through the natural laws of God. Since Jesus' crucifixion his spiritual consciousness is now, far greater evolved than when he was on earth. There has never been on earth, anyone through whom the manifestation of the spirit has been greater than through Jesus of Nazareth. *There also has never been any through whom the laws have revealed themselves as so great an intensity as through the Nazarene.* S. Birch

Jesus showed us through his example how we could use our psychic and spiritual powers to expand and increase peace and happiness on earth. Jesus never contradicted or took advantage of any psychic or spiritual laws. Jesus was the master of these in his understanding of their operation, though his humanity sometimes came to the forefront. Read Mark 11 on this, where Jesus gave us the assurance that we can do the same and that whatever we believe in our hearts, we can manifest; even if it is to cast mountains in the sea. Mark 11.23 ...*and shall not doubt in his heart, but shall believe that those things which he said shall come to pass; he shall have whatsoever he said.*

We have limited knowledge of his life because the records are insufficient, but from the recordings that we do have, the value of Jesus' life on earth was to be an example of humility (humbleness and modesty) for us to follow. John 21.30 says that Jesus performed many other mighty works that were not recorded. Jesus does not want us to worship him as God. We cannot limit God, for God is everywhere. He personally proclaimed that there is only one that is superior and that is God. Mark 11.18 *Why callest thou me good? There is none good but one, that is, God.* In Matthew 22.37, he said *Thou shalt love the Lord thy God with all thy heart, and with all thy soul, and with all thy mind.* Verse 38 *this is the first and the greatest commandment.*

Jesus at his time has revealed the power of God to His children; he has spoken the language of their day. The Bible is full of metaphors and you cannot take every word literally. The revelation/exposure was adapted to the demands of their day and age and in the country in which they have lived, to the stage of growth and development of the people in that time. Jesus taught on the level that was suitable so that the people were able to understand his teaching in that time. His teachings were always simplistic and not too high or beyond the reach of anyone. His teachings, were also applicable to that period. Confucius was the inventor of the golden rule, though Jesus taught the same rule more than five hundred years after Confucius's death. *Therefore, all things whatsoever ye would that men should do to you, do ye even so to them: for this is the law and the prophets.* Matthew 7.12.

As the eras evolved and changed, so did the teachers. New teachers arose, new seers, new prophets and new visionaries, each with his vision, mission, dreams, prophecies, message, inspiration, truth, and his teachings adapted to the needs of his day and age. There is no finality in revelation, for our Creator is perfect. The revelation of today is the revelation of yesterday; Jesus did not deny the truths taught by Moses for example. Jesus quoted the *Ten Commandments* in Mark 10.19. Because the people of today are of a higher stage of development, the truth that God reveals to us has to be more progressive as the truth that was revealed to the people during the ancient times. The important fact is that *Truth* is *Truth* and it is consistent and unfailing.

God has equipped us with the same inspiration that He bestowed on earlier civilizations and on the old masters, saints and sages such as Plato, Confucius, Silver Birch, Aristotle, Buddha, Gandhi, Mohammed, and Jesus of Nazareth. All of us can receive the same inspiration from God that Jesus obtained from God. You do not have to go back more that two thousand years to the time when Jesus lived to be able to receive God's gifts. God is here now. Jesus came to fulfill the law and he did nothing contrary to the natural law. All his actions and teachings were part of the law. He said *All these things shall ye do and greater things than these shall ye do.* What does Jesus say? He demonstrated what we all could achieve when we allow the fullness of God's Spirit to reveal itself in our lives.

You have to use your own reason; he said not all the words that they say Jesus said, afterwards the 'creedsmen' had added many of the words. We have to understand that the same spirit, the same inspiration, and the same great force of God which made Jesus the Great Master that he is, is waiting for us, if we are prepared to open our hearts to receive it from God. Because you are a tiny part of God, all His love, power, wisdom, knowledge and truth are waiting for you, you only have to open your heart and collect it from your Creator.

We have to follow Jesus' example and give help, support and relief through kindness to all. He always promoted peace, joy and happiness. Surely Jesus must be sad when he sees that all his people, followers and ministers close their eyes to all the disgrace in the world of today. He came to show us that we have to help the poor, uplift the sad, heal the sick, give a tired soul a place to sleep, give food to the hungry and we have to awaken the world to put things right where they are wrong. Jesus taught us that we must do the things of his Father, which is our Father. He also said *not every one that said onto me, Lord, Lord, shall enter into the kingdom of heaven; but he that doeth the will of my Father which is in heaven.* In Luke 6.46 he said *And why call ye me, Lord, Lord, and do not the things which I say?* It is only what we do, that counts; - we have to follow the example that Jesus gave us.

Jesus taught us not to accept and tolerate war, starvation, poverty, injustice, misery, unemployment, wickedness, evilness and any form of wrongdoing or sin. He showed us how to live in harmony with God's laws, how to attract and use God's gifts for the greater good and how to live a life of virtuous living through promoting peace, forgiveness and harmony and by giving love and service to humanity, especially the poor and to our enemies. *Generosity is not giving me that which I need more than you do, but it is giving me that which you need more than I do.* Kahlil Gibran. There is virtue in loving and giving to those you do not like. Jesus taught us that love is the greatest power in the universe and that love is fulfilling the law. This love is the motivating power to break down the barriers between substance and spirit, which means that love conquers death. Jesus demonstrated this when he rose from the *dead,* and when people saw him in flesh after his *death.* Read Luke 24.49 when Jesus promised his disciples that he will give them the same special gift from his Father. *And behold, I send the promise of my Father upon you: but tarry ye in the city of Jerusalem, until ye be endued with power from on high.* Resurrection is part of the law of life. Resurrection comes to every soul when it resurrects from your human body when you die and when your spirit, moves on to the next plane of eternal life.

God's promise to you is that the power that has guided you so far on your life's path will continuously guide you, and it will never abandon you. God's power itself is with you; your guardian angel and all your angels' helpers are with you. This power is incapable of failing. When Jesus prayed in the garden of Geth-sem'-a-ne before his crucifixion, legions of angels ministered to him and they were there to strengthen him in his hour before his crucifixion, Matthew 26.53. He also told Peter that he could call twelve legions of angels to help him, if he chooses to. He taught us through his example that in the midst of the *dark night of the soul* when you feel that you are at wit's end, that's when you can hear God's voice, the angels' whispers and experience your Creator's total unconditional love.

We have to learn to cultivate confidence, trust, faith, peace and tranquility within to create the perfect conditions for the divine power to be able to enter our hearts, minds and souls. Jesus endlessly emphasized through his teachings, that it is his Father's divine love, which makes the universe possible, that guides the universe and all who live on it. Jesus was during his earthly life the reflection of divine love. It is through this divine love that members of the human family feel compassion for one another, which enables them to help those who are close to them, their family members, and those who are not related to them. Jesus taught us to serve those who are less fortunate than we are, through divine love, which should always be the inspiration. He showed us that it is easy to love those we love and there is no virtue, or goodness in that, but when you help someone that you do not love, the value, feature and characteristic that you portray is that of a developed soul. Below are some examples on virtuous living that we can learn from Jesus' teachings:

- **Faith**: Blessed are those who believe and have not yet seen, but thrice blessed are those who know and, because they know, place their faith in that which they have not yet seen. Read

Luke 10.24.

- **Virtue**: Live lives of unselfishness towards humanity with the desire to help through compassion, humbleness, kindness, grace and love. The only way to develop self is to forget self. The more you think of others, the better self you will become. Read Mark 10.42-48

- **Love**: Love everyone with warmth and sincerity without alternative motives and not thinking of yourself and expect no reward, such love describes the divine in action, thus it is love expressed through mercy, compassion, kindness, humanity, goodness and grace. Love your enemies, do good to them, which hate you and bless them that curse you, and pray for them which despitefully use you. Whenever you are confronted with an opponent, conquer him with love. Read Matthew 5.44, Galatians 6.13 and 1 Corinthians 13.

- **Judgment**: You have to be merciful, as your Father also is merciful. Jesus taught the laws on the principle of what you do, you will get in return (cause and effect): We must not judge or condemn and we have to always forgive. Read Luke 7 on this.

- **Seeds are true to their nature** - so are people: A good tree will give good fruit and we recognize trees by its own fruit. When a man's heart is good and honest, he will reflect honest and virtuous deeds, a man who has an evil heart will act accordingly which will result in evil deeds. Luke 6.43

- **Power over death** – Resurrection is part of the law of life. There is eternal life beyond death. *If you them be risen with Christ, seek those things which are above, where Christ sitteth on the right hand of God.* Colossians 3.1 This shows that God is eternal and the operation of His laws are unchallengeable, that even as one (Jesus) was resurrected, so are all resurrected, because resurrection is a law of God - God is life. We all have to pass through the gateway of death and leave our human bodies behind to begin a new eternal life in the realm of spirit. Luke 24

- **Serve and Worship** – Jesus' example was to always be humble and kind *whosoever of you will be the chiefest, shall be servant of all,* Read Mark 10.44. He said about himself: Mark 10.45 *For even the son of man came not to be ministered unto, but to minister' Jesus told us that God is the only one that we have to worship.* Luke 11.27 *Thou shalt, love the Lord Thy God with all thy heart, and with all thy soul, and with all thy strength, and with all thy mind; and thy neighbor as thyself.* Our Creator is the life force; He is the vitality, the energetic, the dynamic and the mainspring of all existence and we have to serve and worship only Him. You have to be like a candle, which illuminates a dark room, only by example can you show the way. *Let your light so shine before men, that they may see your good works, and glorify your Father, which is in heaven.* Matthew 5.16.

- **Prayer** – You have to pray with your heart, soul and mind, and it must be a true spiritual exercise, mere requests are not prayers. When your prayer is from your soul and a prayer of earnestness and aspiration, a prayer that desires to reach out to God then the very desire gives it wings which carry it into the heights of the realms of spirit. *Therefore I say unto you, what things soever ye desire, when ye pray, believe that ye receive them, and ye shall have them.* Luke 11.24.

Jesus came into the physical word and he fulfilled the first part of his mission to emphasize a few straightforward spiritual truths. Jesus, Plato, Francis of Assisi, John Wesley, Kahlil Gibran, Gandhi, Socrates, Voltaire, Confucius, Aristotle, Buddha, Mohammed, Silver Birch, and Benjamin Franklin to name a few, as well as all the other Lightworkers of the world, showed us through their teachings that the world does not need some high-flow, theological, abstract collection of doctrines. The world of today needs a few elementary, simple spiritual truths; these truths are the essentials for all religions. We are describing *religion* as a service to all and not the building or institution and its leaders and dogmas. These authentic spiritual teachings, were inspired by Spirit, and were taught in earlier periods. Spirit also inspires today's teachings. These truths are valid in today's life as they were earlier, such as, that the entire human race is part of one another and that beneath our physical differences we have a common bond of the spirit, which unites us all. The *Truth* that we have experienced so far is the perfect concept of spiritual thought and action; it is a splendid enlightenment, an unwavering endorsement of integrity, moral courage, virtue, ethical conduct and service to God, man, and every living thing. We are all members of the same family of which God is the Father because He is the universal nexus of all life. We have to cultivate our hearts to acquire and enhance fundamentals such as brotherhood, service, forgiveness, toleration, teamwork, humanity, co-operation, friendship and love. We have to learn to build on these fundamentals, and to serve and desire to help one another, and to love one another, until we do so; there will not be peace. We have to see the underlying unity and apply the fundamentals in our own lives, then we will provide the kind of existence that God intended us to have. We are all the same under our skins; prejudice, discrimination, racism, bigotry and injustice of any sort are wrong. Our goal must be to treat everybody as unique individuals. As Albert Einstein said: *the world is a dangerous place. Not because of the people who are evil; but because of the people who don't do anything about it.*

I watched the 1982 Richard Attenborough, Gandhi DVD on Mohandas Karamchand Gandhi 1869-1948, and was inspired by his spirituality. The Indians gave Gandhi the name Mahatma, meaning *The Great Soul*. Gandhi believed that violence could never be the way to achieve any objective. *To forgive is not to forget. The merit lies in loving in spite of the vivid knowledge that the one that must be loved is not a friend.* During the last few minutes of his life just before he was killed by one of his own people, he made a profound statement that the only devils around, were the devils that people themselves carry around in their hearts. Sadness came over me and I wondered if he could have sensed the profoundness of his words seconds before he was executed. This cruel act highlighted his foresight and wisdom on shocking and wicked crimes that were committed in the name of religion. *The most heinous and the most cruel crimes of which history has record have been committed under the cover of religion or equally noble motives.* As a messiah of peace and non-violence Gandhi tragically died at the hand of violence.

Pease considered being the true ruler of all values. Genuine happiness only emanates when your soul and mind are at peace.

We have to choose to make the world a better place. Then we can cultivate the fruits of spirit, which is love, joy, peace, longsuffering, gentleness, goodness and faith. - Galatians 5.22. To me, Galatians 5.1-26 is one of the most beautiful passages in the Bible. If we would be able to follow these few basic principles daily, it is possible to live a virtuous, *perfect* life. Choose to be a Lightworker.

In everyone's life, at some time, our inner fire goes out. It is then burst into flame by an encounter with another human being. We should all be thankful for those people who rekindle the inner spirit. Albert Schweitzer 1875- 1965, Alsatian theologian, musician, philosopher, and physician.

Chapter 20

Virtue Intelligences - Values and Principles

Few will have the greatness to bend history itself; but each of us can work to change a small portion of events and in the total of all these acts will be written the history of this generation.
Robert F Kennedy

Virtue intelligence is our intuitive and learnt ability to watch and monitor and to restrain and moderate our natural social behavioral patterns, which includes how we act and manage others. When we develop our virtue abilities well, it will allow us to take advantage of our strengths and skill intelligences in understanding our true passions without harming others. Our actions will portray effectiveness, power, energy and influence through gracious behavior. You can be powerful and gracious at the same time. If you do not know what your truest interest is, you have to search for mentors that can uplift and help you to find your passions through implementing your talents virtuously.

Keep away from people who try to belittle your ambitions, small people always do that, but the Really Great make you feel that you, too, can become great. Mark Twain

You have to choose to be a great person through carrying out virtuous actions.

Virtue Intelligence Trees

I don't know what your destiny will be, but one thing I do know: the only ones among you who will be really happy are those who have sought and found how to serve.
Albert Schweitzer

We can distinguish two distinct virtue intelligence trees. The first determines the wellness and potency of the individual and the second manages the relations between individuals and helps people build fulfilling and harmonious relationships.

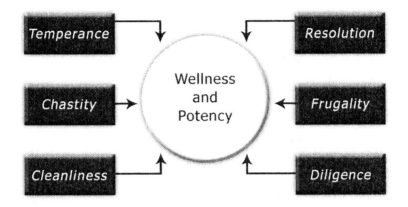

Virtue Intelligences that Determine Wellness and Potency
Virtue intelligences that secure and build our personal wellness and potency.

The words of Benjamin Franklin are used to explain the meaning of the words.

Benjamin Franklin dedicated himself to the clarification of virtues and devoted a significant part of his life to this cause (Franklin P125)

Benjamin Franklin was a printer, author, philosopher, statesman, scientist, inventor rated on equal footing with Newton and rated in some respects as the greatest man the American continent has produced. He is rated as the philosopher who did most to extend the rights of man over the whole world. (*Readers Digest* – Great Lives Great Deeds – Bruce Bliven – P389)

Virtue intelligence Influence

Temperance – "Eat not to dullness, drink not to elevation, avoid extremes, forbear resenting injuries so much as you think they deserve." When we avoid excesses and extremes of any kind in the consumption of food, drink and other consumables we maintain the internal balance and harmony required for sustained wellness.

Chastity – "Rarely use venery but for health or offspring, never to dullness, weakness, or to the injury of your own or another's peace or reputation." When we avoid excesses in sexual activity we reduce the risk of exposure to diseases, interpersonal conflict and creating dependencies.

Cleanliness – "Tolerate no uncleanliness in body, clothes or habitation." When we strive for personal cleanliness we reduce the risk of contamination and infection to ourselves and others.

Resolution – "Resolve to perform what you ought to and perform without fail what you resolve." When we deliver on our promises to ourselves and others, we establish inner and mutual trust.

Frugality – "Make no expense but to do good to others or yourself; i.e. waste nothing." When we work wisely and sparingly with our money and assets we are in a position to help others who are in need.

Diligence – "Lose no time, be always employed in something useful, cut off all unnecessary actions." When we invest our time in useful work and ensure that we do it in the most effective and efficient way, and so that we receive fair compensation for our effort, we can help people who need help.

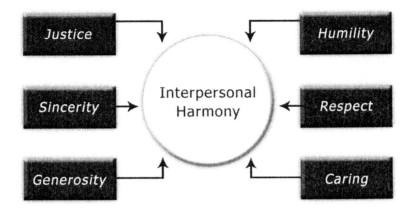

Virtue Intelligences that Determine Interpersonal Harmony

The words of Benjamin Franklin are used to explain the meaning of the words.

He dedicated himself to the clarification of virtues and devoted a significant part of his life to this cause (Franklin P125)

Virtue intelligence Influence

Justice – *Wrong none by doing injuries or omitting the benefits that are your duty.* When we avoid and decline unethical and illegal opportunities and refrain from knowingly harming people, we protect ourselves from adversity and injury.

Sincerity – *Use no hurtful deceit, think innocently and justly and if you speak, speak accordingly.* When we are sincere and just without deceit in our interactions and dealings with people, no harm or injury will come to our loved ones and ourselves.

Generosity – *Give to the needy.* When we are kind and give to the needy we will receive blessings and kindness beyond our wildest dreams.

Humility – *Avoid arrogance and overbearing pride.* When we are humble, people will see and experience the strength in us, more so than when we are arrogant.

Respect for dignity – *Nurture the dignity of others.* When we nurture the dignity of another person we grow the inner true spirit of that person.

Caring – *Love they neighbor like thyself.* When we care about people as we would like them to care for us, we live according to the golden rule.

Source: Words in parentheses are by Benjamin Franklin in his autobiography of 1784

Rest assured that by honoring God's laws and by living a virtuous life, that God will protect you. *There hath no temptation taken you but such as is common to man: God is faithful, who will not suffer you to be tempted above that ye are able; but will with the temptation also make a way to escape, that ye may be able to bear it.* 1 Corinthians 10.13. It is our responsibility to live and walk in the Spirit, which means that Spirit guides all your actions. When you need assistance, call on your angels, the beings who radiate the great light of God, they are full of wisdom and understanding, mercy and tenderness, and they know everything even before you express it, they know your innermost thoughts and they can see the workings of your mind, they know your successes and your failures.

Twelve Indispensable Values to Ensure Virtuous Living

We may realize and understand how in the sphere of spirituality, the most famous and beneficial people in the world are not those that carry titles, money, wealth and power but those who are imbued with a set of qualities, virtues or values. In all the known practices of spiritual wisdom, we are expected to meditate often on these indispensable directives. Noble spirituality emphasizes the fact that such values do, as a matter of fact, empower our lives. The ability to foresee consequences before you act is the mark of a profound person.

The greatness of human beings is attributed to the kind of spiritual life we lead and not to the titles we carry and the wealth we possess. We have to walk our talk meaning practice what we preach. We have to do what we know is right and let our *higher self* emerge in our life. Always strive to obtain knowledge and service, which are greater than fame, wealth or any individual. Below are the great spiritual assets and universal links that we find in all religions. For spiritual refreshment you have to contact your higher self through silence by taking a few minutes out of your busy schedule to reflect. By reflecting on the basis for a virtuous life and honoring the laws of Spirit you will find bliss, aliveness and peace. The first three values are the desired states of consciousness, emotional bliss and aliveness caused by the nine values that act as drivers and levers.

1. **Peace is the paramount ruler of all values**. True happiness emanates when our mind and soul are peaceful. You are peaceful when you know that you are one with your Creator. You are at peace when your heart beats as one with God's great heart and when your will is at one with God's great will, and when you are one in soul, mind and heart with your Creator.

2. **Contentment hails as the embodiment of all values**. Buddhist teachings encourage individuals to clear themselves from any kind of desire to be able to achieve a genuine state of inner peace and joy. When you through your own free will allow your inner self to develop, your mind will crave for spiritual nourishment and you will focus on eternal realities and not on your physical foundation. You will enhance your soul-growth and your focus will not be on the temporary joys and desires of your physical senses. To be truly content means that the desire among all will be to serve one another and to live in harmony and peace.

3. **Cheerfulness vibrates as the evidence of all values**. Clearly as the sun rises each morning after darkness, cheerfulness is the pure joy after we had experienced sadness and pain. When you

radiate cheerfulness you focus on the positive and in return you receive joy in abundance. Cheerful individuals have a tendency to be constructive in all their thoughts and actions. Making people cheerful is viewed as a heavenly blessing.

4. **Courage functions as the heart of all values.** In Christianity this quality is considered to be one of the seven gifts of the Holy Spirit. It requires courage to put the knowledge and truths of spirit into action. Apply service and unselfishness to every-day affairs in your life thus you will be able to attract peace, harmony, unity and friendship. Through such a virtue good can triumph over evil, justice can triumph over injustice, and right can triumph over wrong.

5. **Truth forms the foundation of all values**. In Christianity Jesus declared: *I am Truth*. Truths do not change which is based on knowledge that comes from God. Truth is constant and eternal and when truth is appreciated and understood in the fullness of its implications your soul has moved out of darkness into the light. No knowledge can alter truth and we have on earth the fundamental truths to require our essential purpose to give service, kindness and love. We know what we should do to have a better world.

6. **Respect is acclaimed as the demonstration of all values**. A fundamental virtue as seen by several ascetics is when we demonstrate respect for others, which we show through expressing love. Saint Augustine the father of Christian education stated this profound wisdom during the ancient times *Love and do what you want*. When one's actions are love based you thrive to live a nobler life, a life of greater self-sacrifice and optimism that will demonstrate your Creator's hallmark on all your actions. Live the reality to *Love thy neighbor as thyself* as Jesus showed us.

7. **Humility is honored as the protector of all values**. Our Creator accounted those who serve others as the great souls. By giving service to others you are tuned into the highest

vibrations of Spirit, and through you Spirit's work can go on. The virtue of humility is acting out the priceless knowledge of the truths of Spirit in action. Every single one of the greatest saints of all time was characterized by their humility. The only way to develop self is to forget self, the more you think of others, the better self you will become.

8. **Reflection is identified as the key of all values**. The quality of our conscience is that part of our soul which discerns between right and wrong. Our conscience is the pointer of our soul. It enables us to reflect periodically on our actions and thoughts for self-examination to improve our spiritual life. Life consists not only of the things we do, but also of the things we say and the things we think. Through silence we can reflect on our words and thoughts, which are part of us, and we can learn to master them. Set aside a little time each day to retire into the silence of your being and your soul to allow the power of spirit to rise to the surface. You can manifest the spiritual forces within and without when you are quiet, receptive and subdued.

9. **Simplicity is deemed the great beauty of all values**. Many years ago Jesus taught that *A little child shall lead them*. Until we learn to put away the foolish wisdom of the wise, and get back to the simplicity of the child, we will not advance much either on earth or on the spiritual plane. We have to view the world through our spirit eyes and realize that our sprits are all one, and linked with the unifying spirit of our Creator.

10. **Patience is heralded as the fortress of all values**. *The reward of patience is patience* Saint Augustine. The virtue of patience is restraint; with patience one will achieve everything. Eagerness can dampen the vibrations and atmosphere when we want to achieve results quickly. When we master complete passivity, peace and quietude we will easily manifest results. Develop the habit of practicing silence with the intention to enhance your ability to give love, service, harmony and goodwill; in

return you will be blessed with the beauty of this quality.

11. **Honesty is proclaimed the guru of all values**. Our aim and desire to be of service must be based on honesty and noble virtuous intentions. When our motives are honest with the purpose to serve, we will be capable to win the hearts of all people we come in contact with. Individuals are able to sense honesty without exception. Practice integrity, be authentic and experience how people warm up towards you. When you practice genuine interest in the welfare of people you win their trust.

12. **Purity is branded as the mother of values**. Only our Creator is and can be truly pure, perfect and supreme, we can only strive towards being pure and perfect. Our tiny portion of Spirit is perfect and pure but not our manifestation in our physical form. For this reason we have the processes of evolution which goes on without end throughout all centuries. Our evolution consists in the refining, in the purging away of the dross to allow the gold to become exhibited, in cleaning imperfections away from the innate perfection. The secret in life is that you have to have perfect balance between your spirit, mind and body. All great leaders of the religions of the world had attached great importance to the purity of heart, mind, soul and body. You are fulfilling yourself when you allow Spirit to manifest in your life. Your responsibility is to be as pure an instrument as you can be for the power of spirit to flow through you.

What to do next, how do you find your way?

With ease and confidence, honor the golden rule.

Do not unto others what you would not have them do unto you.
Confucius

You have to respect life, people, the animal world and the environment. You have to value life through honoring God's laws and by applying virtues and values. You can only accomplish mutual understanding through the recognition and appreciation of the unique nature of each human being. There is only one path to fairness and justice in the physical world and that is respecting and embracing uniqueness. Your motto must be to have *reverence* of life, which will result in honoring God's laws and to respect all individuals, to show consideration and to value individuals and their unique abilities. When you truly understand, it means that you acknowledge without judgment and that you admit to the various facets of reality. When you treat individuals with respect, you will attract conciliation and mutual respect from other individuals. Individuals can sense when one's heart and intentions are pure. When you value the uniqueness in others, they will warm up to you and union will take place. This union will result into joy.

How do you know that you know?

The irony is that we all want the same thing – think about it – what do you want? We want to feel appreciated and we want people to love us for who we are. We want recognition for our own unique abilities no matter how small they are. Now that you know that the thing you have been searching for truly exists, the search becomes easier. You are also aware that all individuals are searching for the same thing. You have to give to others what you in fact want (and need for yourself) and you will receive in return from them what you want through your giving. We all want to feel wanted and loved. Now that you have seen your objective, reaching it is just a matter of finding your way through life's experiences and challenges. To be able to receive you have to be able to give something in return. We are back at Jesus' command: *Whosoever would save his life shall lose it, and whosoever shall lose his life for My sake... shall save it.* We have to give sincere, passionate, loving service to humanity; but we must always be careful in the grip of passion not to hurt anyone. Unrestrained, fiery emotions are the essence of being alive. Through applying and honoring God's laws, we can make a difference today in someone's life and we can grow our souls through virtuous living. Stand your ground, even if it means that you have to stand-alone, and you will reap the rewards. Do not follow the fads of daily temptations. When you follow the flavor of each month, it will be impossible to be a unique version of yourself. You will always try to win someone's approval and in the process lose yourself. You will drift on the mighty ocean as if you are a small vessel and the wave of the day will take you away, or even worse, the biggest wave will consume you and you might drown in the process. Be bold and have only two forthright affirmations: To honor God's laws and to live a life of virtues. Write a ceremonial note of yourself as if you were dead; use the words that ALL people will use who know you such as your friends, and your so-called enemies. What do they say? This can be a challenge – fix whatever you do not like. *I cannot and will not cut my conscience to fit this year's fashion.* These were the wise words from Lillian Florence Hellman. When I move on to the next plane of life, I would want people to say that about me; meaning of course, that I will not compromise my integrity for anything. I will also not look the other way when I see hardship, unfairness, injustice or any wrongdoing. Now you have to make a choice. Choose a life where you practice and portray a life of integrity, moral courage, virtue, ethical conduct and service to God.

The Challenge - Emotions and your state of being

There is a continuous war in the physical world we live in between the enlightened and the darkness of ignorance. When you are happy and open-minded, you are positive and life seems to be easier than usual. When we are content, we experience bliss. We cannot always be on top of the world. Think back about the parallel roads that we have discussed in the first part of our book..

Passion is the state of our emotions; you can be passionate

about anything, choose wisely that which you want to pursue. Because our emotions are unrestrained, they can tell us more about ourselves that our thoughts can. Our emotions and intuition will give us guidance on our state of being.

Always remember that when you are going through a difficult period that your emotions will experience darkness within, which will result in sadness. Everything around you can be perfectly bright but because your emotions are out of control, your hormones will be out of balance and you will experience feelings of turmoil. When your emotions do not flow, they hurt and you experience a stand still. We experience severe feelings through trauma. Trauma and distress can sometimes hide for years and then strike swiftly like a snake. Its venom is the unwanted emotion that immobilizes us. When the unwanted past pushes itself into the present you have to overcome the present and move on to your future. Focus on new beginnings and on your bright future. The next paragraph can help you to change your mindset. Affirm the following:

I .... can tackle and handle any matter that arises and comes my way in perfect stillness and with an attitude of acceptance without animosity, anger and disgruntlement, in order for my growth to be uplifted to another level of consciousness. I will be able to sustain my level of attitude with whatever is shown or thrown to me, so that I talk and walk in absolute TRUTH, and understanding. And I will see and believe what I do is for the Highest Good and Purpose in my life so that my heart is opened to receive and put in the good and worthy energies for me to live my life in peace and harmony and balance. This will give me the strength to pursue, persevere and perceive whatever comes my way as exciting and as a new chance to talk and work through the challenges as a new project and with enthusiasm. So: - I bless the universe for the changes taking place in my life in order to grow and to move on and up to higher planes of consciousness. - So that the works and mechanics can be worked on, and done with TRUST, knowing all is according to the Divine Plan of Action taking place in my life, and for that I am grateful!

Always be in charge of you – justice and soul- growth is flawless through cause and effect.

Those who can make you believe absurdities can make you commit atrocities. Voltaire 169-1778 - French Enlightenment writer, essayist, deist and philosopher.

You are aware that you have to prepare for eternity and you have to grow your soul. When you die, your soul will start its new life at the level of development that it has attained. Your soul cannot be higher or lower than what it is. The natural law takes cognizance of every factor. What you do and think while you are on earth, you register on your soul. You reward and punish yourself through your actions. You grow, or fail to grow, because of your own life. Albert Camus (1913-1960) a French-Algerian author, philosopher, and journalist who won the Nobel Prize in 1957 said: *Do not wait for the Last Judgment. It takes place every day.*

We have repeatedly highlighted the fact that you are in control of yourself. Before we conclude our book I have to stress once again that through the natural law justice is perfect and flawless. Because only you can register your own spiritual growth, the natural law will determine your fate through your actions. This means that every individual is in charge of his own fate through God's natural perfect laws. You are what you are; you cannot pretend what you are not. Whatever you do on earth you register on your soul. Your soul is richer or poorer for what you have done, because YOU have made it so. Ponder on the wise words of Albert Einstein; *the significant problems we face cannot be solved by the same level of thinking that created them.* Make a decision today to change your thinking to a higher level of consciousness. Be in control of you and change whatever is out of balance, teach your consciousness to discover the creative light within, which will give you the insight to find your unique creative powers and talents. Live in the present and exercise virtue in all of your actions. All good things are the result of inspiration, motivation and thought – seeing your intentions through until they manifest. Through identifying your unique personal strengths, by developing it and by bringing it forth, your creations will bear fruit. The joy of virtuous actions and mastering your creativity will result in personal reward and enrichment of your soul. When you put effort in and create with love, you will experience God's approval through receiving love from others and rewards from the universe. Transform yourself from within by living a virtuous life in terms of the natural laws. Visualize, pray, have faith and believe that you are in control of you. Again, have faith like a little child Luke 18.17 *Verily I say unto you, Whosoever shall not receive the kingdom of God as a little child, shall in no wise enter therein.*

The following true story is of my 21 year old Lizél at age four.

Excitement was in the air for it was the pre-school 1991 Christmas celebrations. My first born, Lizél was waiting for Santa Claus. She experienced all the fun and activities of the day with wonder. As the occasion was also a fundraiser, the main event was a draw consisting of an exquisite fine porcelain toy tea set decorated with flowers and butterflies. Lizél saw the tea set and through the eyes of a child she immediately fell in love with it. We purchased a ticked whereby she asked me why they didn't hand us her tea set. I explained that it was only a ticket and that they will have a lucky draw at the end of the day. She asked me what she had to do to ensure that she would get the price. I immediately thought that it was a golden opportunity to teach her about visualization and faith. I told Lizél to visualize in her mind that she wins the tea set. The four year old asked: *What is visualizing mommy?* I told her that she has to see and believe in her mind that the lady will pick her name among all the other names in the hat. I also told her that she must hear how they call her name out as the lucky winner. She was pleased and confirmed that she will do just that. Lizél's father was furious, there were approximately a hundred and fifty kids. He told me that I was irresponsible for the odds were slim. What would I tell her when she hadn't win, he asked? My reply was, I don't know but then I will have a plan B. Maybe tell her someone needed it more than she did, I will address the problem when we have a problem. At that point the most important thing was for her to learn how to visualize and to have faith. Every now and again she would confirm that she is visualizing and asked if that is all that she needed to do. I then told her that she need to say thank you for winning the tea set and then enjoy playing with her new tea set. She and her teddy bears have to drink from the tiny teacups. By the end of the day Lizél and her imaginary tea set was inseparable. At 16h00 that afternoon everyone gathered around for the lucky draw. The teacher's hand disappeared into the big black hat and we all waited in anticipation. Lizél's father was looking at me with piercing, *I told you so* eyes. My heart was jumping, as suddenly I was not feeling so good, I remembered that I thanked God in advance for His miracle but was scared to death. Then the teacher called out Lizél's name, needless to say that it was NO surprise to her. We on the other hand were amazed and relieved. Until this day Lizél's father cannot believe that faith from a four year old could have been so powerful. God is great! Visualization is a reality and with God and dedicated faith, miracles do happen. *Unless you become like little children you cannot enter the kingdom of heaven.* Find and expand your inner-child, trust your childlike instincts and intuition. View the world through the eyes of a child and you will find God.

Conclusion

To be free is not merely to cast off one's chains, but to live in a way
that respects and enhances the freedom of others.
Nelson Mandela

You are a *Special Being from the Light* and you are aware that you can achieve whatever you desire. You can and you will make a difference to yourself and to others by reflecting on the basis for a virtuous life and honoring the laws. When you transform yourself, you willingly go through a physiological change of one thing into another, such as when larva goes into adult through metamorphosis. Now you are able to find the inner peace within you and you are able to connect so that you really get to a stage in your life where you feel at peace with yourself and others. You are now at a stage in your life where you are not afraid of the ups and downs of life, as you are aware that it is part of the natural cycles of life. Through finding spirit within, you find peace, love and spiritual truths and you are able to focus with eagerness and joy on what you do have and not on what you do not have. Through this transformation, you are preparing yourself with the makings of new changes and happenings so that you are now able to stand your ground well balanced. You have awakened from the chrysalis (cocoon), which you have used as a shelter until now that you are able to refresh your mind with clear thoughts and find within you the inner peace with love and healing. You as a Spiritual Being from the Light can transform yourself into the exquisite butterfly that God intended you to be. Through the connectedness of the highest power, you have the wisdom that it will carry you through in whatever you do and wherever you go. Experience the challenges and adversities in your life as beautiful stages of growth that contribute to your soul-growth. Have affirmations that will uplift you and help you to reach new levels of consciousness and put a smile on you face and open you arms and receive whatever God puts on your path. Know that your new level of consciousness can only get stronger and stronger and that all your challenges are for your highest good and purpose to grow and to prepare yourself for eternity. When you have concert, rhythm, balance, harmony and wholeness between your mind, body and spirit you will have peace with God, the world, everybody in it and most importantly, with yourself. You accomplish this through honoring the natural laws, giving service to your environment, nature and humanity and by living a virtuous live. When you fulfill yourself, you are allowing your Creator to manifest in your life. You will very soon find that in giving out to another you will receive back abundantly. By giving out love, you receive love and you help to heal the world. Shine your delicate light and illuminate the world – choose to be a Lightworker and be like a little lighthouse that sends beams of truth sharing knowledge to souls which are still in darkness!

Rely on yourself and be a living example of following one's Divine Guidance through giving help, service and teaching to others. You do not need to transform the world, when you help and uplift one soul you have justified your existence. Aspire to give service on an ongoing daily basis. Always act with optimism and faith, and listen to Divine Guidance - your inner source of direction, which is within your thoughts. When you need direction, alter your thoughts. The solution you seek is born within your thoughts. Ask your Creator and listen in stillness for direction of your thoughts to support you during your time of transformation.

All you need is love! The fruit of the Spirit is love and God is within you. Your responsibility is to be as pure as you can be. Your goal has to be to always be in control of yourself and to filter all your thoughts through your heart with love before they become actions. When you can master *the self*, you will reap the rewards. Self-mastery is an ongoing process of trail, error, adversity and victory! You are always on the road of discovering who you are and growing within. Soul- growth is eternal. You always have a higher level of evolution to grow towards.

Listen to the song *All you need is love* by the *Beatles* early in the morning before you start your day, ponder on the words during the day and choose to be happy.

Chorus:

All you need is love, all you need is love,
All you need is love, love, love is all you need.
Love, love, love, love, love, love, love, love, love.
All you need is love, all you need is love,
All you need is love, love, love is all you need.

Now you can change the world! With love in your heart – you can change the world! Love is stronger than blood and death. Love is the permanent force because love rules the universe. The real meaning of love is that love in essence is God. 1 John 4.8 *He that does not love has no knowledge of God, for God is love.* Love is the quality that binds minds and souls. Always give service with love, affection and devotion and increase your character with the eternal hallmark on your soul. My final thoughts to you are that God is your strength and your heaven – read Psalm 55.22 *Cast thy burden upon the LORD and He shall sustain thee: He shall never suffer the righteous to be moved.*

You are the seedling and you need to nurture, care and love yourself to be able to grow towards heaven. Soon you will be able to flourish. When you enter summer, you will be able to attract butterflies, bees, insects, and proliferate your seed to manifest new seedlings. Burgeon into the beautiful rose that you are and share your exquisite fragrance with humanity... Trust your Creator - let God be the warming sunlight in your life and choose to illuminate the world with your light. I am closing by leaving you with the words of Bette Midler's beautiful song *The Rose*.

The Rose (lyrics)

Some say love, it is a river, that drowns the tender reed
Some say love, it is a razor, that leaves your soul to bleed
Some say love, it is a hunger, an endless aching need
I say love, it is a flower, and you, its only seed
It's the heart afraid of breaking, that never learns to dance
It's the dream afraid of waking, that never takes the chance
It's the one who won't be taken, the one who can't seem to give
And the soul afraid of dying, that never learns to live
When the night has been too lonely and the road has been too long
And you think that love is only for the lucky and the strong
Just remember that in the winter, far beneath the bitter snow
Lies the seed, that with the suns love in the spring becomes the rose.

I wish you only love and blessings on your way forward. May you find Spirit within and may you experience God's love daily. I truly wish that all your dreams became a reality!

And whatsoever ye do, do it heartily, as to the Lord, and not unto Men;

Knowing that the Lord ye shall receive the reward of the inheritance.
Colossians 3.23-24

Practical Exercise: Use Faith and Prayer as a powerful tool to manifest blessings into your life.

Don't face the day until you have faced God. Maya Angelow

When we receive help, guidance and knowledge from above we have to share it with others. The following process has helped me to manifest blessing into my life. Use the process below to place an order with God to manifest spiritual, mental, physical and material blessings into your life. The truth is that you can manifest whatever you desire through the realization that God's power is within you. Faith works hand in hand with the process of *Divine Timing* that has an incubation period. When we pray, we sometimes have to wait for certain things to develop before the manifestation can take place. Compare your desire to a seed that you plant, you have to grow, nurture and love your seedling before it grows into a tree that produces fruit. Just as you have faith and know that it will produce fruit, have faith and know that your desires will manifest.

FAITH is the process of turning your desires into reality

Follow the four basic steps below
1. Visualize a clear goal and result
2. Engage in a burning internal desire
3. Pray for certainty
4. Articulate and demonstrate your anticipation and happiness with your reward

Visualize a Clear Goal
First you have to *visualize* what you want. Imagine the crystal clear picture of exactly what you want, now develop and write a detailed order in ink. Place your order with God. The passion of

seeing what you want gives you the burning *desire*. Make a 10-point list on what you want. Describe this in detail. Put the list up where you can see it (make a separate list for every goal that you have).

Engage a Burning Internal Desire

Read your 10-point list out aloud first thing everyday when you wake up before you do anything else. Do the same at night before you go to sleep or when you meditate and ponder the importance of your goal and convince yourself that the goal will change your life.

Pray for Certainty

Pray on this goal everyday until you experience the feeling of certainty in your heart. All goals have an incubation period, pray on your specific goal until you have the certainty that the time is ready for you to receive this goal or thing.

Articulate and Demonstrate your Anticipation and Happiness with your Reward

Demonstrate your faith by telling people that you already HAVE attained this goal. Believe that you will receive the things that you cannot yet see. Demonstrate this faith by seeing it in your mind's eye and talk about it enthusiastically. Enjoy the manifestation of your goal in the energy centers of the body, feel the ecstasy in your mind. Thank God in advance for answering your prayers.

IMPORTANT: Always remember that in faith there is always a *Divine Incubation Period* that must lapse before you attain your goal. The clearer your goal, the more you pray and the more certain you are, the shorter this incubation period becomes.

For example: When you pray for a partner or soulmate you have to be 100% specific and clear of what kind of husband you want. There are millions kinds of men.

Below is an example of a list of ten specific points. You have to make up your own list.

1. What race/ ethnic group? White, Black, Indian, Greek, Portuguese, Italian etcetera
2. Height - Do you want a short or a tall man, thin or plump etc
3. Hobbies? Music, art, athletics, sport, philosopher, etc
4. What age group?
5. What occupation? Teacher, engineer, lawyer, gardener, preacher etc
6. What colour hair and eyes – blond and blue eyes etc
7. Is he a sensitive man or a robust man?
8. Is he your soulmate?
9. Is he passionate or disengaged?
10. Is he spiritual or non-spiritual?

Bibliography

Alington C.A. Rev, The New Standard Encyclopaedia, Odhams Press, 1936

Andrews Ted, Crystal Balls and Crystal Bowls, Llewellyn Publishers, 1995

Birch Silver (Edited William Naylor), Anthology, Ebenezer Baylis and Son, The Trinity Press, 1955

Birch Silver (Edited Storm Stella), Philosophy of Silver Birch, Spiritual Truth Press, 1969,2004

Die Bybel (Nuwe Vertaling), Bybelgenootskasp van Suid-Afrika, Nasionale Boekdrukkery, 1983

Holy Bible (Dictionary Concordance), King James Version, Thomas Nelson Publishers, 1977, 1984

Hornby A.S, Oxford Advanced Learners Dictionary of Current English, Oxford University Press, 1974

Joubert Belinda, AngelSense, Kima Global, 2006

Joubert Belinda, Nature Virtue Cards, Protea Playing Card, 2007

Joubert Danie, Talent Management, Knowres Publishing, 2007

Kritzinger.Schoonees.Cronjé.Eksteen, Groot Woordeboek, Engels.Afrikaans, J.L. van Schaik, 1926,1994

Krafchow D, Kabbalistic Tarot, Inner Traditions, 2002

Levin Michal, Meditation, Dorling Kindersley Ltd., 2002

Merriam-Webster A, Webster's Third New International Dictionary, Merriam-Webster Inc., Publishers, 1986

Spencer Lewis H, Self Mastery and Fate, The Rosicrucian Press, Ltd., 1929

The Bible (Authorized Version), The Bible Societies, Oxford University Press, 1978

The Reader's Digest Association, Great Lives, Great Deeds, The Reader's Digest Association Ltd., 1965

The World's Popular Classics, The Autobiography of Benjamin Franklin 1790, Books, Inc. Publishers, 1867

BOOKS

O is a symbol of the world, of oneness and unity. In different cultures it also means the "eye," symbolizing knowledge and insight. We aim to publish books that are accessible, constructive and that challenge accepted opinion, both that of academia and the "moral majority."

Our books are available in all good English language bookstores worldwide. If you don't see the book on the shelves ask the bookstore to order it for you, quoting the ISBN number and title. Alternatively you can order online (all major online retail sites carry our titles) or contact the distributor in the relevant country, listed on the copyright page.

See our website www.o-books.net for a full list of over 500 titles, growing by 100 a year.

And tune in to myspiritradio.com for our book review radio show, hosted by June-Elleni Laine, where you can listen to the authors discussing their books.